The **Women Who Won**

WOMEN _of the_ 27TH DÁIL

by

Úna Claffey

Attic Press
Dublin

© Úna Claffey 1993

First Published in Ireland in 1993 by
Attic Press
4 Upper Mount Street
Dublin 2

British Library Cataloguing in Publication Data
A catalogue record for this book is available from the British
Library.

ISBN 1-855940-736

Cover Design: Syd Bluett
Origination: Attic Press
Printing: Guernsey Press

Attic Press gratefully acknowledges the assistance of the various
party press offices and individual TDs in supplying the
photographs contained within this book.

Contents

Preface

The general elections of November 1992 saw an unprecedented twenty women elected to Dáil Eireann. The historic decision to appoint two women to the cabinet and three women to junior ministries followed in the wake of that general election. This high number of women deputies was welcomed by all those who wanted to see equality in Irish society, but it still leaves Ireland way down the European league table for female representation in national parliaments. In Denmark 33 per cent of parliamentary deputies are women, in Holland 28.6 per cent are women, in Germany women deputies account for 20.5 per cent. While Ireland is not the lowest in the community (that dubious distinction goes to Greece with 5.3 per cent) with just over 12 per cent it has a long way to go before a critical mass is achieved. The magic figure needed for this is thought to be eighty-four, that is the figure which would give women a majority of one in the Dáil.

Since their election some of the twenty women thought it would be a good idea to come together in a loose formation to discuss issues of interest to them as women deputies. They decided to call themselves Group 84. Their first action as a group was to meet the Tánaiste Dick Spring to highlight the programme of systematic rape of women in Bosnia. There are mixed feelings amongst the twenty TDs about such a group, ranging from the view that women should not separate themselves from their male colleagues to the view that says fundamental political differences will always separate them. The group received some adverse publicity but there is a feeling amongst the women that mutual support is necessary.

As the number of women deputies increases so too does the level of conciousness about how difficult it still is for women to be elected into Leinster House. The difficulty stems not from the electorate who have shown they will vote for good women candidates, but rather from the obstacles encountered by women as they battle through what are still male-dominated political parties. More than one of the women in this book comments on how difficult the process is for women especially those women from out-side Dublin, those women with young families, and women who have a small income or none at all. However, it is interesting to note that, in current analysis of what a party needs if it is to improve its vote, high profile women and possibly even a woman leader are at the top of most pundits' agenda.

There are common threads which run through the profiles in this book. Many of the women come from political families and it is interesting to see how in most cases the daughter and not the son won the Dáil seat. None of the twenty women Dáil deputies is the partner of a former TD. All of the women come from homes where equality of opportunity for daughters and sons was the norm. In a sense these women's stories give a glimpse of how the role of women in Ireland is evolving. However, representation of women in the Dáil has risen and fallen in the past. Perhaps the election of Mary Robinson as President of Ireland has marked a fundamental change and we will continue to see the representation of women increase. Much will depend on how these twenty women acquit themselves and if they can convince other women that the sacrifices they speak about in this book are worth it.

Úna Claffey
March 1993

Mary O'Rourke

First elected to Dáil Eireann:
February 1982 — Fianna Fáil

'I remember one morning, waking up in the flat and saying, "I'm not going in. I'm pulling the duvet up over my face and head and I'm just not going in." That lasted for about an hour and a half, but then I hopped out of bed and said, "Okay, put on the paint and away you go." ' That was Mary O'Rourke's lowest moment, one week after the

Taoiseach Albert Reynolds fired her as Minister for Health. She readily admits it was a huge crisis in her life.

She had been regarded as a highly successful Minister for Education, had just recently moved into Health and loved it. 'Immodestly I thought my record would stand to me.' She had absolutely no inkling that when Albert Reynolds took over from Charles Haughey as Taoiseach she would not be in his cabinet. Neither had anybody else. The others who lost their positions had been well flagged she said but nobody expected either herself or Gerry Collins to be sacked. In hindsight, she says, perhaps she should have expected it.

She first heard the rumours in Leinster House. She was then called to the Taoiseach's office. She remembers thinking, 'It's not going to happen to me,' and saying so. She said she felt absolute disbelief until she stood in front of him and he said to her, 'You won't be in the government.' She was determined to take it well and simply said, 'Thank you.' She was going to have her hurt in private and with her friends, not in the Taoiseach's office. She turned on her heel but as she reached the door he asked her if she was interested in Máire Geoghegan-Quinn's job. (She'd been Junior Minister for European and Women's Affairs before Haughey sacked her.) Mary O'Rourke said she'd think about it.

It was just half past three and the Taoiseach was about to nominate his cabinet for the approval of the Dáil. She sat in the back row of the chamber with her colleagues who'd been fired. There were gasps from the press gallery. She describes it not so much as a public humiliation, but as a very public disavowal of her years of service. She felt it wasn't happening to her. What helped was the fact that there were seven others with her. When she looked at people like Gerry Collins and Rory O'Hanlon, whom she describes as having 'minded the pass' for years, she felt, 'If he's let go, and he's a good guy, it's not that there's anything wrong with me. I'm just part of some scene.'

Mary O'Rourke went over to her department to collect

her belongings and says luckily her husband Enda and son Feargal were there. She had a 'fat gin' and ranted and raved. She cried a little in the department but really cried that night when she got home to her flat and let her anguish out. She talked it over and over with friends and didn't sleep all night. She came in to Leinster House the next day but found it very difficult. She had a call from the Taoiseach but told him she wasn't interested in Women's Affairs. She doesn't think women's affairs should be separate from all other affairs.

Albert Reynolds then asked if she was interested in a job, to which she replied she had been the day before. Their conversation was brief but very tetchy. At the same time she felt there was a reaching out to her and out of her instinct for self-preservation she told him she'd like something in the economics sphere. By that evening he rang her back and said, 'Trade and Marketing. I think you'll do fine in it.'

Being fired was her second major defeat in a week. She'd stood for party leader against Albert Reynolds and got a dreadful vote. That didn't affect her half as much; she hadn't really expected to win and wasn't too disappointed. But being fired was a total shock.

'Politics is my life,' she says. But while very content with the course of her life at present, she's restless. She's never content with just knowing that today's work is done. She wants to know what's on the next day. She doesn't know what she's restless for. She's very pleased with her assignment as Junior Minister at the new Department of Enterprise and Employment. Surprisingly, she *has* now decided on one very important thing. She will never be Taoiseach. 'My time has gone, age-wise. I'm fifty-six in May,' she states emphatically, closing the subject.

When Mary O'Rourke confronts a crisis she talks. She talks to herself, she talks to her family and she talks to close friends, but essentially she talks to herself. She goes over things in her mind especially when she wakes up in the morning. She asks herself what she's going to do, is she going to be able to cope, to behave with dignity. But she doesn't think she could cope without a partner; a contented family background, that's what gives her security. The fact that her husband Enda was there, physically, with her after she was fired and that her two sons were at hand was crucial.

Enda has been there for almost everything in her life. She met him when she was eighteen and he's been the great love of her life. They were, she says, very much in love, 'very physically in love'. They married at twenty-two and even today their passion is not all spent. Mary says she is a very tactile person and notices men, their physique, and how they look. She doesn't think that politics de-sexes a woman. She doesn't feel that she intimidates men at her present political level. However, she says that earlier on, at county council level, when she was in her early thirties, she was aware of this but she put it down to professional envy more than anything else. She admits that it's harder for women to get on in politics. She feels now that she's very glad that she did her political apprenticeship when she did and that her children were twelve and sixteen when she went into national politics.

Mary O'Rourke could never get enough of politics when she was growing up. She describes herself, 'ears out listening, listening'. It seemed to her to be an exciting world in which all sorts of unexplained, unexpected things could happen. That remains the same for her today. Her father was the local party man in Athlone. He was, as she says, plucked from the civil service by Seán Lemass in the late thirties and asked to set up a cotton factory in Athlone. He was to be the managing director; there was to be a board of directors and the state was to be the main shareholder. It was part of the interventionism of Lemass in attempting to build an indigenous industrial base. General Textiles Limited employed a thousand workers at the height of the operation, most of them women, and they worked three shifts. The Lenihans lived on the factory site in a former protestant preparatory school, and Mary says she grew up to the sound of the factory horn going off every eight hours. Her father was a good businessman but a bit of a poet and dreamer.

Mary was born shortly after her parents came to Athlone, five years after her sister and seven years after her eldest brother Brian. There were four children. She says she was a nuisance. She wanted to go everywhere they were going and was constantly tagging after them. When they were teenagers they hated being told to bring her to the cinema. They had to bring her to get their pocket money, but would then try to dump her when they got up the town. She was always trying to keep up and wanted to be their age immediately, to be doing what they were doing, straight away. She wanted to be at the action, even then, although she was far too young. Their parents made no differences between their sons and daughters. Mary says her parents were never just husband and wife. They were two people with separate identities. Her mother was very much a person in her own right. She played on the Irish bridge team and had come first in the country in French and History in her Leaving Cert. Mary's maternal grandmother had been widowed when she was in her late twenties. She had six children and twelve acres in Co. Sligo. She was particularly keen to educate the girls and three of them went to university.

The Lenihan household in Athlone was very liberal. There was no such thing as 'not in front of the children', everything was discussed and she says she had to 'run like mad' to keep up with the others. When she heard conversations that she didn't understand she would rush off to look up dictionaries and find out what people were talking about.

Perhaps it's not surprising that she was lonely at boarding school in Loreto Bray. She loved the academic side but says she was exceptionally lonely. Lonely for Athlone, lonely for home. She was five years at boarding school and never went back there at the beginning of term without being lonely. During term she was always dying to get out of it. She says she can still feel the sense of desolation when she went back, although she was very fond of the nuns and teachers in the school. She had two aunts in Dublin who used to visit her; she can remember pathetic phone calls to her father when he came to Dublin on business and tears when he came to see her.

She speaks quite openly of her feelings of inadequacy in her early teens. She became quite introspective, worrying, cautious and doubtful. She distinctly remembers being unhappy, having conflicts within and finding it difficult to adapt to things. She describes herself then as 'difficult and prickly'. Her sister was quite different and she remembers people in boarding school saying, 'Oh, you're not a bit like your sister.' Mary went to University College Dublin (UCD) at the age of seventeen. Her father had suggested a BA to her but she told him she didn't want to teach. She was interested in a career but felt she'd like journalism. Her father pointed out that there were very few women in journalism and suggested that if she did the BA it would be a very good foundation for whatever she wanted to do. She was adamant that she didn't want to teach but says she was lucky that her father could send her to college without a proven career in sight. Ironically, she subsequently did teach and loved it.

Mary and Enda married when they were twenty-two, although both sets of parents thought they were too young. Enda was earning enough to get married and it all seemed very simple. Mary's father gave them a site in Athlone. They built a house on it and they are still living there over thirty years later. She remembers getting a county council loan. The house cost £2,200, the loan came to £1,600, there was a grant of £200, so they had to make up £400 which was huge then.

After her marriage she longed for a child, but didn't become pregnant. Her brothers and sister were all married and produced one child within one year, two children in two years and three children within three. Year one went by, year two went by and year three went by for Mary and

Enda but there was still no child. It was a period of her life when she can distinctly remember being distraught, unable to come to grips with not having a child. They were two very healthy people with a good physical relationship, no inhibitions and they couldn't understand what was happening. She says she became obsessive about it. Her father saw this and suggested she consult Dr Eamon de Valera, the gynaecologist.

The very next day she got Dr de Valera's number, made an appointment and was off on the train to Dublin. He advised her that she had no medical problems but said she was worrying too much. He then asked to see Enda. 'That would be quite normal now,' says Mary, 'but it wasn't then.' She has always thought that Enda's response was tremendous. 'There he was from provincial Ireland. He didn't blink an eye. We went back to the doctor together to discover that Enda had no problems either.' She remembers Dr de Valera putting his hand on her arm and saying she would have a child, she mightn't have very many but she would have one. She wondered subsequently if he knew something about her that he didn't tell her.

By now, she says, Enda had become infected with her desperation for a child. Within six months she became pregnant. Her memories of Feargal's birth are graphic. 'I can still recall the physical thrust of having him; the push.' Her only regret is that she didn't breastfeed him. When she suggested it to the nurse she was told, 'Nonsense, I've your bottles all made up.' She never had the pleasure of breastfeeding because her second son is adopted. After her marriage, the finest thing, and the most wonderful thing to ever happen to her, was to have her two children. Four years after Feargal's birth she adopted six-day-old Aengus. The three of them went to Dublin to collect him.

It's the public side of politics that Mary O'Rourke loves most of all, the Dáil, the performance. She says she's not power-hungry but she's not afraid of power either. She's not interested in the trappings of power. Big cars don't interest her; most days she walks to work. She remembers her feelings of elation and then trepidation when she was made Minister for Education in 1987. She recalls thinking about the department, the staff, the budgets, her worries about those issues. But she was very interested in education and wanted to 'get at it'. She gave it an awful lot of work. She quickly established a good rapport with the unions, who had been at loggerheads with the previous coalition government, recognising that they each had their own agenda, and she says both sides very quickly got on to a good working relationship.

Apart from running her own department she loved the overview of government she got while in cabinet and says she was a very active participant. Even at the worst of times she has never thought of giving up politics — at least she has never considered it for longer than an hour and a half!

Niamh Breathnach

First elected to Dáil Eireann:
November 1992 — Labour Party

Within days of her appointment as Minister for Education, Niamh Breathnach came under fire. With the agreement of her constituency colleagues she appointed her daughter, Clíodhna, as her Dáil secretary. Clíodhna knew the constituency as well as her mother, and was totally familiar with her filing system. They had worked perfectly as a team prior to Niamh Breathnach's election to the Dáil. It may be the minister's first taste of controversy about decisions she takes; it is unlikely to be her last.

Coincidentally, Niamh Breathnach's father, Brendan, was a great supporter of another person who became a minister on his first day in the Dáil – Noel Browne. 'There were pucks of politics at home. My father was a Clann na Poblachta man,' she says. Her mother's family were from Clare. They supported Fine Gael, but Niamh never knew this until she met an uncle years later who was chairman of a branch of Fine Gael. She remembers her mother, Lena, had terrible memories of an incident in the Civil War involving two brothers on opposing sides. Niamh says her mother didn't express political views when Niamh was growing up. Both her parents were civil servants and Niamh is the second eldest of five girls.

Her most vivid memories of childhood are linked to music. She was born into a world of music where her father played the uileann pipes in the kitchen, her mother went to the women's sodality for a night out, and she and her sisters got into devilment upstairs. She remembers how her father would disappear if he heard of a musician dying in Kerry. He'd get someone to drive him to the station with a heavy tape recorder, and he would then take the train so that he could record the dying musician's work, for posterity. Her father, she says, didn't feature much at home. Her mother was the authoritarian figure who regulated the five daughters.

She recalls how her father was opposed to corporal punishment. He was an extraordinarily gentle man. 'If anyone was going to take a side swipe at you, it was my mother. And we could run faster than she could.' In many respects her father led a separate life; he had his own group of pals with whom he went for a pint in the local. But her memories of his domestic life include recollections that he washed dishes on Christmas Day, took them into town on Christmas Eve to count the lights, made mashed potatoes for them in the shape of their initials when their mother was in hospital having babies. Her mother used to say he got away with murder.

Niamh says he was an Irish man of his time. While her mother was from Clare, her father came from silk weaving stock in the Liberties and grew up in Donore Avenue, Dublin. He moved through Synge Street to the civil service and was determined to educate his five daughters. His attitude was: they would get no dowry but they would get an education. He wanted them to stay in school until they were twenty-one. The question of marriage was not an issue when she was growing up. Niamh had no sense that she would *have to* marry and settle down. She doesn't know how her parents managed to pay for the education of five daughters since there was no free secondary education at the time.

Both parents expected their daughters to do well at school and there were no rewards for passing exams. Niamh says she was bright and was in the A stream in primary school. She was articulate and middle class. The philosophy at home was to work hard. Your best wasn't always good enough. 'I know that when my school reports came in, I sometimes took myself off to town to hide.' If you worked hard the belief was you generally got what you wanted. It wouldn't fall into your lap; you didn't battle against other people but you worked hard. It was a happy home in Dublin's Blackrock where the Breatnach family lived and indeed where Niamh Breathnach still lives.

In the 'sixties Niamh went to tennis club dances. She travelled to London and brought home clothes from Biba's, probably the most famous 'sixties boutique. She loved to rock and roll but says she never learned to do *real* dances. When she goes down the country to Labour Party functions and an old man wants to do a foxtrot she has to say she's 'too young' to do that. She describes herself as giddy when she was growing up but says she had a best friend who was ten times more giddy! She recalls how she met her husband. She was going out with an American marine who'd come to live in Dublin. The marine, who wore a coat like de Valera's, had gone home for Christmas. Niamh was at a party and was doing the washing up. She needed someone to help and woke up a guy who was asleep behind a couch. She discovered he had an odd sense of humour and started to go out with him. They were at the Abbey to see *The Borstal Boy* when she decided she was going to marry this Tom Ferris. She says she was attracted to him because he was sensible, unlike the American marine who went around dressed like a French Lieutenant out of the Napoleonic Wars. It was a wonderful marriage, she says. She was by then a national school teacher. Tom's parents thought he was too young to marry but were happy that he was marrying a teacher. They have two children, daughter Clíodhna and son MacDara who is doing his Leaving Certificate this year.

Family life is very important to the new minister. 'When I win the most extraordinary battles I don't want to go on the town. I want to go home. I have that thing about wanting to go home. But sometimes you go in the door and they're all asleep.' Occasionally, if she's very tired she likes to take a day off and stay in bed. She likes to read women's magazines. It's her way of 'switching off'. She never buys them. But if her children want to know what she wants for her birthday, it's *Woman's Journal* to read Katie Stuart on cooking, and *Cosmopolitan*. She admits to reading the transcript of the Prince Charles tapes before looking at another story in that morning's paper. She read everything about the Bishop Casey affair. It knocked her back, she says. Speaking of religion she says, 'I need God more than God needs me.' She talks to a Being out there. She prays to a God.

Niamh Breathnach has her own unique way of dealing with disappointment. She plants things in the garden. The lavender bush went in after she lost the election for vice chairperson of the Labour Party. She doesn't kick the cat and she doesn't cry when things don't go her way, but she is quite capable of cursing under her breath. Some people say Niamh Breathnach is bossy and pushy. She says it always surprises her to hear this but if that's how they think it doesn't bother her. It does take her aback, but then she says she *is* a school teacher.

Niamh Breathnach insists that all she wanted to be was a deputy for Dún Laoghaire. To be Minister for Education she says was beyond her wildest dreams. However, neither was she mesmerised by her appointment. She had been involved in student politics but dropped out when she married. She resented the fact that when she came into the Labour Party in her thirties there were those who said they couldn't support her because she wasn't long enough in politics. Her reaction was. 'Blast you. I went home and you didn't.' She thoroughly enjoyed her years at home. She listened to Radio Four and Woman's Hour and Marian Finucane. She heard Kate Millet and Mary Robinson. For her it was a great time to be at home and reading. Joining the Labour Party, she says, was her first experience of being in an almost exclusively male society and she found it very difficult because she was expected to keep her mouth shut. She was taken aback when it was remarked that she had spoken at her first meeting. 'Why wouldn't I speak? I was thirty something years of age.' The fact that she spoke at her first constituency council meeting was interpreted as 'having ambitions'. She does feel, however, that she came into the party at the right time. It was through listening to Labour Councillor Mary Freehill speak about the Labour Party that she decided to join. She has a theory about one's moment in time. 'You grab it,' she insists.

Niamh expected to take a seat in Dún Laoghaire in the general election of 1992 because she felt such a constituency had to return a Labour candidate. But she found the speculation about her nomination to government very stressful. She'd gone to Connemara with her family immediately after Christmas. She was driving across a bog road when she heard the *Sunday Press* political correspondent Stephen Collins saying on the radio that she was going to be made a minister. In the family it became known as 'if' and no-one was allowed to talk about it. The day the Dáil convened she sat in the front row in dirty boots because it was snowing and she'd just been outside for a photo call. She was in her Dáil office changing her boots when Dick Spring walked by. He spoke to her husband who was waiting for her in the corridor but simply greeted Niamh. Later she and Tom walked towards the stairs. The Party Press Officer Fergus Finlay came after her, put his arm around her and told her Dick Spring wanted to speak to her. That was the moment, she says, which was her wobbly bit. She felt something significant was about to happen. She was told of her appointment at ten past five.

Had she not been nominated she feels it would have been hard to take, especially for her supporters, because of all the media speculation. Her nomination, she feels, was Dick Spring's vote of confidence in her. She's not worried about the fact that when you start at the top the only way ahead is down. At forty-seven she says she is dealing with people who are more important than she is and younger too. She says she's the only one who is aware of her age and that people laugh when she mentions age to them. 'I know politicians can in theory go on for ever, but I think, like the Bishops, they're beginning to retire a little bit earlier.'

Liz McManus

First elected to Dáil Eireann:
November 1992 — Democratic Left

'I'm not in politics to shore up the *status quo*. I'm there to change, to transform.'

For many people Liz McManus would seem the most unlikely person to join a left-wing party. She is by her own admission 'well heeled and articulate'. Her early years were years of privilege and comfort, in a home where there was a daily maid, a home that held no clue to how radicalised she would become. But Liz considers it very logical for her to be in Democratic Left. She says she sees no conflict at all and often asks other people why aren't *they* in Democratic Left. Her sense of injustice is keen and while she recognises that others may respond to this in a variety of ways, for her, politics *is* the way. She sees a crucial role for her party in forcing political change and genuinely sees no alternative if justice is to be done.

Liz McManus's origins are far from the world of politics. She describes the existence of her family as 'peripatetic'. She was born in Montreal, moved to Switzerland and then France, but her first real memories are of Blackrock in Co. Dublin, before her family moved again to Holland where her father, Tim O'Driscoll, was the Irish diplomatic representative at the Hague before Ireland established full diplomatic relations with Holland.

Liz is the daughter of a mixed marriage. She describes her father as coming from a very solid Cork burgher lineage. His family were good staunch nationalists. Her mother Elizabeth McKay, however, was a unitarian from the North. 'There was always this difference. It made me feel to a certain extent at one step removed from the traditional Irish upbringing that everybody else had. It made me feel one step apart. This has given me a different perspective to the traditional Irish catholic upbringing.' She was raised a catholic and says she found it difficult to cope with the fact that her mother was not like other people's mothers; she didn't say the rosary and she didn't go to mass. Even though Liz went to schools which she says would have been progressive she was told to pray for her mother's conversion. Liz didn't find it offensive but says it was bewildering. 'I knew damn well that nobody was going to convert my mother, even though she didn't proselytise at all. But she was a free thinker and certainly wasn't going to be converted by my prayers'. Her mother had gone to art school and was a painter before she married and although she didn't work outside the home when Liz was growing up, she's now a silversmith. Clearly her strong sense of her own identity, and her determination to maintain it, greatly influenced her daughter.

While there was tolerance in her family, Liz says her parents were not liberal by today's standards. She and her two sisters (she is the youngest in the family), were expected to be 'ladylike'.

There was no political discussion in the O'Driscoll household. Her father was always travelling. He had literally gone round the world three times before she was fourteen, had helped establish Foynes as an air base and was a passenger on the first ever Aer Lingus flight. Other people's fathers only went to Manchester, she says, while hers brought home extraordinary presents from places like San Francisco. 'Other people's fathers brought home Spangles (British sweets not available in Ireland at the time) but my father would bring home chocolate-covered baby bees.' It was very exotic.

One of the unexpected delights for Liz McManus at age forty-five is the very close relationship she enjoys with her parents. She does not remember any deep personal or intimate conversations with them when she was growing up. She was, she says, a bit of a loner, very shy and quite withdrawn, partly because her sisters were four or five years older than her and they had left home quite early. At school she was considered to be aloof but says she can see the same characteristic in one of her own four children. She describes it as a feeling of separateness.

The question of religion did bother her at times in her life. She couldn't accept simple statements that, for instance, it was a sin to go to Trinity College Dublin (TCD), that protestants weren't part of God's elect, because in her own home there was a protestant who quite clearly was as good as anybody else. She had difficulty with these notions. But she describes the nuns who taught her at Holy Child convent in Killiney as a liberating force because they were very forthright, very keen to see girls achieve and presumed girls to be as good as boys. 'They were very strong formidable women, good role models.' When she was elected to the Dáil her old maths teacher, whom she hadn't seen for years, wrote to congratulate her. She recounts this with obvious pleasure.

Liz McManus does not remember any great happiness as an adolescent. She describes herself as dawny, very innocent and very vague. But already she had started to write, something which was to become central to her in later life. There were no great clashes with her parents. She was a good student, more the academic type than sporty. Because of her height she played netball but says she was terrified of hockey. 'There was no way I was going to go out and get myself beaten up by hockey stick wielding girls. That was not for me.'

She had little sense of what she might do when she left school and says the idea that she might determine her own destiny came very late to her. She tried her hand at dress designing which she describes as a total disaster but tells how she judged the guy who sat beside her in class: 'He's equally as bad as me.' 'Years later he turned out to be Richard Lewis the designer,' she laughs. 'I remember a terrible old yellow thing he was making; it took about six months. He probably still can't sew but he can certainly design, which is more than I could ever do.'

After a spell as an *au pair* in Paris Liz went to University College Dublin (UCD) to do architecture, again influenced by her mother. Liz claims she wasn't any good at architecture and that work wasn't her primary motivation for being at university. However, she did qualify without any difficulty.

UCD appears to have been a real turning point for her. To many people she would appear to have led a charmed existence. She never had to deal with any form of hardship. There were no great crises in her early life. She loved being in a very small minority of women in a class of predominantly male students and she certainly had no difficulty finding boyfriends. The care-free days continued when she went to Montreal in Canada during EXPO 1967 when she worked in an Hassidic Jewish neighbourhood close to the Greek part of town where French, Greek and Hebrew were the dominant languages. It was her first real break with home. It got her out of Dublin and the sheltered life she had lived there. She travelled to Billings, Montana, on a greyhound bus and met cowboys in a part of America which was far from fashionable. 'Everyone wanted to go to San Francisco, put flowers in their hair and smoke pot. I was quite frightened by all that. I was there in the 'sixties but I was one of the ones for whom the 'sixties didn't really happen.' Having travelled across the states she thought she'd like to stay in Boston. Her mother felt differently about this and so Liz returned to Dublin.

By this time she knew architecture was not for her, but she persisted with it. She also had her first direct taste of political action. 'The school of architecture was the place where the whole gentle revolution started. (The gentle revolution was the period in UCD in 1968/1969 when students occupied the university. Mass meetings and demonstrations were held in an attempt to achieve fundamental reforms in the way in which the college was run.) It started purely out of self interest. Students got very upset that their qualification would not be recognised any longer by the Royal Institute of British Architects because the standards were so poor.' She attended the first of the hundreds of mass meetings which were to take place in UCD in 1968. Students faced up to their professors and lecturers, demanding change and higher standards. In the middle of one meeting Liz left to go to the loo. To her utter amazement she was followed by the other students who interpreted this as the signal for a walk out. Inadvertently, she says, she was a leader.

She was drawn into the activities of the Dublin Housing Action Committee and remembers being lifted off the street by the Gardaí during a protest on O'Connell Bridge against the appalling housing conditions of Dublin in the late 'sixties. This was a real turning point for her. The same impulse that she felt then still drives her now. A deep sense of injustice. 'In a way, the fact that I came from a comfortable background forced me to face the fact that other people had so little and had been deprived of so much. The idea that even the essentials of life, like a roof over your head, were being denied to people, was a personal affront to me.'

She regarded her student political activities as not being really serious — until she went to Derry in 1969. Her future husband John was going to Letterkenny to take up his medical internship. Liz took a flat in the Bogside, worked with eminent architect Liam McCormick and joined the Northern Ireland Labour Party. She arrived in Derry just after the Battle of the Bogside. She describes as great timing her arrival after the ferment of politics in UCD to the even greater ferment of politics in Derry. She's critical of some of the positions she adopted in politics then, seeing them as very nationalist. She sees her attitude to non-sectarianism then as very simplistic. In retrospect, she feels that a lot of the views she then held are untenable. She was extricated screaming and kicking from Derry when she married John McManus and they moved to Galway, again, because of his job as a junior doctor.

She joined Sinn Féin and stayed with the party through its changes in the 'seventies and 'eighties to Sinn Féin the Workers' Party, the Workers' Party and, finally, when the majority of the Workers' Party split to form the Democratic Left party. After many years in local authority politics both on Bray Urban District Council and Wicklow County Council, she was elected a deputy for Wicklow to the 27th Dáil. Her husband John stood for election in this constituency in the past, but failed to capture a Wicklow seat.

Liz McManus is an extremely practical person. Even as a mother of four children Luke (20), Ronan (19), Sam (16) and Emily (11), she is also an active politician, a creative writer and journalist; she was never missing when her children came home from school, until she was elected to the Dáil. She talks of her marriage in very down-to-earth terms. For the first few months she was in Galway, she knew no-one, she lived on the docks, where she said she watched the sea rise as the rain lashed down and her husband was out working. 'I knew that if I could survive that I could survive anything.' There's a touch of the shared obsession of politics in her marriage, she says, but both she and John take a very practical view of their relationship. 'Because there were never huge romantic clouds that were going to dissipate and reveal some ghastly truth behind them, we went in with our eyes open and our marriage and love has strengthened over the years.'

Having her first baby was the beginning of the biggest love affair of her life. She was besotted by motherhood and felt no great desire to have a career. Once more her husband's work was a determining factor in her location as she helped him establish a general practice in Bray. After the birth of her last child, eleven years ago, she did think of returning to architecture, but found that the people she had worked with in earlier years were now being threatened with the dole. In a sense, she says, the recession actually liberated her and at this point she decided to write. The first story she wrote, she describes as appalling, but her second attempt was published in the *Irish Press* and won the Hennessy Award. However, this was, in a way, her downfall because, she says, she then felt she *was* a writer. She produced material and sent it off, then had to deal with the rejection slips. She took rejection badly. 'I said, oh my God, I'm not a writer at all. I've been fooling myself, I should get out of this and go and do something else. I stopped writing. I was such a delicate flower that I couldn't handle rejection at all.' But at a woman's workshop on creative writing she got the spark again and has won a number of awards since. 'I know I am a writer. It's like knowing you are a woman.' Her election to the Dáil will mean she won't be able to write fiction for quite a while, but she says that doesn't mean she's any less a writer. She passionately wants to return to writing. She now needs her fix more than ever.

She resents the notion that writers should not get their hands dirty or should not get involved in social action. There's nothing in politics for her that would do anything other than enrich the creative part of her life.

But she has seen the dirty side of politics too. The day before polling in the local elections in 1991 she describes how she and her husband were subjected to a vicious smear campaign. Two hundred business people and others in Bray received a letter which alleged that she had been 'carrying on' with other men and her husband had been 'carrying on' with other women. It also referred to her children. She was terribly hurt because it attacked her family, who couldn't defend themselves. However, it completely rebounded. People who would never have voted for her told her they were doing so because they could not stand what was done to her. 'We know you and we trust you and we are not going to let this determine our vote except in a positive way,' they said. She is eternally grateful to the people of Bray for their support at that time and she describes it as a triumph of decency.

Dealing with becoming a grandmother was hard for Liz. She describes that experience as being a bit like a death. The death of a child's childhood. She was angry because she felt that her son and his partner were stupid to let it happen. 'Childhood and adolescence mean being free of responsibility. It is such a short period in your life that to end it so early is foolish. At the time, I felt frustrated because I'm inclined to control things but this taught me that I can't control everything. Destiny sometimes determines life. I also learned that at times I should keep my mouth shut.' Whatever misgivings there may have been about her son's loss of childhood, her grandson, Stephen, is now at the heart of her family.

Liz McManus is not certain what her expectations are of Dáil Eireann. She's concerned about the highly centralised nature of the institution and of government. She does not expect that as an individual she will make huge changes. Once again she feels a bit of an outsider. As part of a small party she is proud of what she sees as the cutting edge of Democratic Left, but she acknowledges that this makes her different. 'I don't feel part of the club. I hope that if I lose touch with my roots or the people that I represent or become part of the club I will realise it and I will leave.'

Frances Fitzgerald

First elected to Dáil Eireann:
November 1992 — Fine Gael

For Frances Fitzgerald the November 1992 election could not have happened at a better time. She was the ideally placed candidate to benefit from the upsurge in support for women and being the go-getter she is, she went for it.

She had a very high profile as chairwoman of the Council for the Status of Women (CSW), a position she'd held for four years and from which she was shortly due to resign. She had to decide where to put her energies. There was the possibility of a job in the equality area, or there was the possibility of going into party politics. As chairwoman of the CSW she regularly appeared in news reports leading delegations to government ministers during the Maastricht and abortion referenda. When the election was called she decided, as she says, to give it a whirl. The announcement of her candidature came as no great surprise. Fine Gael had been delighted to nominate her.

She makes no apology for being ambitious and says she'd like to go as far as she can. She'd like to be Taoiseach and doesn't set any limit on what she could do. Career-wise she says that at this stage in her life there is nothing she's ever really wanted to do that she hasn't done.

Frances didn't like her first day in Leinster House and says she wasn't in a celebratory mood about it. She found it very heavy going. 'I think it is in many ways the centre of male conditioning and the effects of that conditioning get expressed here almost more than any other place.' But she has no doubts about her capacity to deal with that. She says she'll do so by getting to know the system, by being well informed, by working very hard and by being as honest as she can about her experiences. When asked if she'll be able to hack it she replied that she doesn't think it's an easy place. She thinks it's a lonely place to be and a hard place for women.

Although aware of how little she's seen in the short time she's been in the Dáil, she's already critical of the style of debate in the Dáil chamber. Her first experiences were the debates on the election of Taoiseach and the government. But the kind of things she saw, the personalised style of debate, the kind of cutting comments made, these, she says, pierce her as a woman. She thinks they probably pierce the men too but they don't show it. She has found positive feelings of support from both her male and female colleagues in Fine Gael. She's very glad that there are twenty women deputies in the Dáil but feels that Leinster House changes women, that politics de-sexes them and that they assume a style of expression that's more male in attitude. There's pressure on women, she says, to become one of the lads!

When asked about her attraction to her husband, Michael Fitzgerald, who is a psychiatrist, she thinks for a while before she answers. They met while they were both working in Dublin's St James's Hospital where Frances was a social worker. After some prodding she says he was calm, warm and then, finally she blurts, 'He was just mad about me.' He's had a profound influence on the course of her life, most particularly when he decided, for career reasons, to go to London and she went too. She decided to go to the London School of Economics but it was Michael who suggested she take a Masters Degree rather than the Certificate of Qualification in Social Work (QSW). He's always been supportive and helpful to her and keeps saying, 'Why don't you?' He has challenged her and she likes this.

She spent the early years of her life in Newbridge, Co. Kildare. Her father was an army officer and she was the eldest with two sisters and a brother. She describes herself as the typical eldest; out there striving, wanting to make a go of things, wanting to live up to expectations. There were six years between her and her brother and ten years between her and her first sister. She'd have loved a sister closer to her in age and feels that the gap made her a bit of a loner growing up. Frances Fitzgerald says she is a reflective person, that she agonises and analyses. She was conscious of being the daughter of a member of the army and of the lifestyle that went with that. It was a restrictive lifestyle and her parents were aware of the opportunities the army had given her father. She says that at an early age she made a realisation about opportunity and the lack of it. As an upwardly mobile family, a lot of the values she saw in her early life were the values of conservative small town rural Ireland. It wasn't a particularly political family although both her parents voted Fine Gael. From her paternal grandfather she got an interest in and love for history, which she has carried with her.

Frances speaks of having a somewhat ambivalent attitude to her mother. She felt that her mother devoted all her energies to the family. Frances feels she should have concentrated some of her energy on herself although she describes her as a wonderful mother. Frances was close to her father. Both parents expected that she would do well educationally. Getting a job and getting married would also have been a central expectation of her. But their expectations were not huge, she says, and she would have preferred them to have been higher. She says it was very hard for parents at that time, and particularly for women, to have huge visions of possibilities because society was so confined. She feels that she learned from her parents about the restrictions of class.

Her early school-days were in the national school in Newbridge but she loved moving to Dublin in her early teens and going to the Dominican College at Sion Hill. The city for her meant openness, potential and opportunity. She'd seen poverty in her school in Newbridge and in rural Kildare and Carlow. While she didn't see it in Sion Hill she has always rejected the accusation that because she is middle class she's not aware of poverty. She was an achiever at school but resents the fact that there was so little attention paid to science subjects. The decision to go to university came early on in Sion Hill, where a lot of her school mates were also going to third level. Social Science was her degree choice. She loved University College Dublin (UCD). Although she was there between 1968 and 1971, she was an observer of, rather than a participant in, the radical politics of the time. She was a party goer, loved student dress dances and played tennis. She herself says she was care-free and, while concerned about getting her exams, found she could do so reasonably easily, a fact which always surprised her. Her placements in social work and a job in St Ultan's Hospital in Dublin sharpened her social consciousness but she describes her response as a one-to-one response. The hard political perspective came later, she says.

The journey to a political perspective began at the London School of Economics (LSE) where, very early on, she moved from the level of individual social work to seeing that such action should address issues in a political way. The process went hand in hand with the fact that because of her husband's career, they decided to wait for six years before having a child. She feels that because she waited and developed her own career she was somewhat ambivalent about having a child and it took her quite a while to decide. She was by now in a senior post in a top hospital in London dealing with children. For Frances this was a most stimulating time. She describes it as being at the cutting edge of thinking and research. It was three years after she started working there that her first child was born.

She loved motherhood. The family came back to Ireland and she breastfed her son Owen for two years (and each of her other two sons, Mark and Robert, for over a year). Frances Fitzgerald dates her interest in feminist politics to this time. She had become involved in London with the National Childbirth Trust. This she describes as her first experience with women-centred issues, women talking about things from their own experience. For her the whole question of childbirth and maternity services was the male world meeting the female world in a most unhappy alliance and there was an awful lot to be done.

Before Frances had her two other sons she had two miscarriages. This was the first time in her life when she went after something and it didn't happen for her. She knew she could get pregnant and didn't get depressed. She and Michael talked about it. She had very good friends and she was living on a housing estate with a lot of other women with whom she was very involved. After the miscarriages and a bit of a wait she did get pregnant again and had two more babies. Frances never contemplated adoption and says she has 'mixed views' about it. Although she loved being at home with her first son she realised that she needed the intellectual challenge of other adults and was nervous that she might not be able to get back into the workforce. She did part-time work until her two younger sons were born and then took a career break for three years.

It was the Women's Political Association (WPA) which brought Frances Fitzgerald into the limelight of the women's movement. She became a member of the association and within a short time was elected chairwoman. Like many women it was motherhood which provoked in her an intense interest in the organisation of society. 'The division of labour really hits you,' she says. She describes this as an intensely political issue. But why did it take her so long to join a political party? It was no secret in political circles that she was seen by many politicians and party organisers as an ideal candidate.

In the particular strands of the women's movement in which she was involved there is neither a history nor a culture of women being highly involved in party politics. And even in the WPA at committee level she says there is almost a kind of veto on party politics. 'I think it's very much a disadvantage. It's not a good idea.' She points to the Three Hundred Group in England where there are Tory women and Labour women involved in a committee and going their separate ways at election time. This she sees as a much better model. She'd like to see that here and feels it's more politically grounded. But she doesn't see it happening – though she has already taken an active role in the Group 84 in the Dáil, where women from all parties are invited to work on issues in a cross-party fashion.

When Frances Fitzgerald decided to run for the Dáil there were women in the women's movement who felt she was careerist and had used her position to promote her own ambition. Frances insists she didn't come across this a lot. She got a standing ovation from the CSW following her election. This gave her fantastic encouragement. 'I think we've got to the stage of maturity where I won't be lashed for personal ambition. What I heard more than anything was "you're very brave". Maybe there is some bravery in standing out and going for election.'

She knows she's been lucky but she's astute enough to also be a little worried. She's used to working with women and has found them very supportive. She's worried about keeping up contacts and maintaining the encouragement she got from other women and the clear vision she's developed and shared with them. But she has no worries about being ghettoised or seen as 'a one issue' person. 'I'm happy to identify with women's issues because I think women's issues are *all* issues and I'm proud to be associated with them.' In spite of whatever misgivings Frances Fitzgerald may have about Leinster House she feels a fantastic sense of delight and pride at having been elected. She describes the election of twenty women as a small step. 'In terms of influencing the agenda or the style of debate it's really only when there are eighty or ninety women that will happen. It's early days yet.

Nora Owen

First elected to Dáil Eireann:
June 1981 — Fine Gael

'Oh for goodness sake call me Garret.' Those were the first words of Garret FitzGerald when Nora Owen addressed him as Dr FitzGerald following her election to the Dáil in 1981. She says she must have shaken his hand somewhere and he had stopped in her constituency of Dublin North on the day before the election, but she didn't really know him. On her first day in Leinster House she was so unknown that Brian Farrell from RTE mistook her for Sheila Barrett (married to Seán Barrett TD). When he told her he wouldn't keep her husband long she quickly told him that she was a deputy too and ended up being interviewed instead of her party colleague. Her seat was a real and unexpected bonus and one that actually put Fine Gael into government with Labour. 'I can remember being up in Ballymun school the day I got elected and the sheer unadulterated joy of the people who had worked for it. It was the first time in my life that some act of mine was causing such great pleasure to so many people.'

But Nora's seat was far from secure and she was one of those who lost out following the collapse of the Fine Gael/Labour Coalition in 1987. Having lost her seat in the Dáil she put on a lot of weight. Her whole sense of her own importance, her status and worth was shattered. 'I woke up every morning saying "God, am I that awful." ' It was a devastating feeling and it didn't matter how much she read about political swings; to her it was desperately personal. She became very irritable and now knows that she was hard to live with at that time. She describes it as similar to having done an enormous injury to oneself, bearing a huge wound and that just had to heal slowly.

She then stood for the Senate but failed to be elected. This clearly aggravated the blow. Between 1987 and 1989 she continued to work her constituency and she worked for her sister Mary Banotti who is a member of the European Parliament. That, she says, was part of a healing process and helped rebuild her confidence. She also became a close friend of Mary for the first time in her life. They'd never really got to know each other growing up.

When Charlie Haughey decided to go to the country in 1989 Nora was determined to stand for election. However, she says, her election at the expense of the long-sitting, former minister and party colleague, John Boland, was traumatic. 'It was clear that I stood a reasonably good chance of being elected and getting a good vote but I always have a terrible sense of doom before an election. I find it hard to believe that four or five thousand people are going to go out and vote for me.' People had been saying to her that John Boland had eased off and that he was studying law, but, she says, it wasn't easy to look him in the face when he was defeated. It was an extremely tense time especially during the count when she was terribly conscious of John, Kay and their children being present. This, she says, is the awfulness of politics. One day you have a job and a salary and the next day the electorate say, 'Well, that's it. We like the look of somebody else,' even though you haven't kicked the boss, you haven't embezzled the funds, you've done none of the things for which you'd normally be fired. One of the awful aspects of losing is that it's so public and that the loser has to help others overcome their disappointment and look bright and breezy, she says.

Nora Owen is a private person. She has a certain stoic quality in spite of her extrovert nature and sense of fun. It may be that her early childhood years have taught her to cope well with disappointment and loss. She doesn't share disappointments easily. This is something in her since she was a child, when she never shared her insecurities with anyone. It has stood to her through the rough times.

She was four and a half years old when her father died, leaving six children under ten years of age. She remembers little about him except an incident one day in the car when her mother asked him if he could see something. He couldn't. He had gone blind. A bank employee, he left his widow with just a small bank pension although she did own her house. She was a domestic science teacher and was just one year below the cut-off age for return to work when he died. She got a job in the College of Catering in Cathal Brugha Street, Dublin. Some people suggested that she might put her children into institutional care but instead she sent the girls to board with the Dominican nuns in Wicklow. Nora was five. She liked school and was happy there. She doesn't know how her mother coped and remembers how her mother would claim that *she* should have been Minister for Finance. Nora suspects that there was some assistance with school fees and she remembers every August, five sets of school uniforms being laid out, darned and mended. That, she says, is probably where she learnt to sew. She wasn't conscious of being poor but is now sure that they were. But there was no time to really get to know her mother, an extremely responsible woman, but very conscious that her family duties should not interfere with her job.

It was only in her late teens that Nora began to develop a relationship with her mother. She herself was not lonely being away, but imagines it must have been frightfully lonely for her mother. School gave Nora a sense of security. She liked its regimentation and says she was a good student. Her mother expected her to do well. She came from a background where girls and boys were considered to be equal and all the girls were educated and had careers. Her mother recognised that what she could give her five daughters and one son was education.

Nora has no recollection of any great family cosiness. There were no visits to Hunters Hotel for afternoon tea like other students had. There was no father to lift her up, as she saw others do. Her mother could usually visit just once a term. She was aware of a kind of gap. She wasn't able to analyse her situation. She knew she didn't have a father and she knew that her mother wasn't an overly demonstrative person, but she doesn't think she particularly suffered. She sometimes talks about those times with her mother, who says she realises that there were probably parts of their lives that they could not share then.

Her mother was a very private person who disliked other people 'knowing her business'. Nora feels her mother must have cried many silent tears on her own, as she wondered how she was going to pay the bills. But she managed; she never went into debt and she paid fees for the four of her six children who went to university.

Nora Owen describes herself as dutiful. Like her brothers and sisters she got summer jobs from the time she was in her mid-teens. She learned early to budget her pocket money in a post office account. She enjoyed college but describes herself as a fairly diligent student. She didn't have the money to be heavily into socialising but she did join college societies and played hockey. She studied science and feels the fact that it was such a male environment has helped her in political life. When she qualified in the 'sixties jobs were plentiful. It was probably the first time that money came easy to Nora Owen. She married her boss, Brian Owen, when she was twenty-two: he was thirteen years older. Brian was then quality manager at Swords Laboratories; Nora was a quality control chemist. When they married in 1968 she moved to research and development with the company.

Looking back, she thinks she was probably too young when she got married. She remembers herself as rather correct and conservative, a person who enjoyed fun but was a bit intimidated because she had never really had a fun kind of life. She remembers these years as a time when there was considerable social pressure on all young women to get married. Having her own home was important to her because of the sense of security it gave her. While she didn't want a family straight away, after four years she began to get worried. She and her husband adopted a son. When he arrived, she found herself pregnant. By 1972 she had two babies both less than a year old. She became a full-time housewife and loved it. A third child was born in 1976. She says she remembers being very relaxed at this stage and quite content to be at home. She is now very glad that she had those years with her children.

Although Nora Owen is a grand-niece of Michael Collins, politics was never discussed in her home and she had no consciousness of him, she says. Yet politics was 'waiting to happen to her'. She had become very active in her community in Malahide in North Dublin. With her youngest child about to go to play-school she was becoming unsettled and knew there were things that she wanted to do. In 1979 the local council boundaries were redrawn and all the political parties were looking for candidates. She was approached by some community council members who were also in Fine Gael. They asked her to stand. Nora says she didn't even know the elections were on. Active politics had never entered her head. Nor had it entered her husband's. He laughed when she told him about the approach and said, 'Oh my God, sure you don't know anything about it.' He too had no political interest, although Nora suspects he voted for Jack Lynch because he came from Cork. But her mother's reaction was quite different. She thought Nora should think about it since she seemed to need something outside the home. Out of curiosity, Nora approached a council official and asked him what a councillor does. 'Well, you know the way you write to me about your path from your residents' association, that's the sort of things councillors do.' Nora figured that if that was all they did she could do it too! It took the mystique away. Her first year on the council was her roughest time but it taught her the system and certainly prepared her for the national stage.

She felt intimidated on her first day in the Dáil. When she sat in the chamber she was conscious of so many people looking at her. The number of deputies had been increased to 166 from 148 and the number of women deputies had rise from five to eleven. She also found it exciting and enjoyed it. She felt she was getting to where she wanted to be. She wanted to participate in Irish life and felt there was something she wanted to do and give and she thought, after her experience at local level, that she might just have a talent for it.

She's come a long way since then. It was she who seconded John Bruton's nomination for Taoiseach in the 27th Dáil; she's a member of her party's front bench and is a senior figure in Leinster house. She would certainly like to be in cabinet but is not absolutely sure if she'd like to be Taoiseach. She knows people regard her as assertive and even bossy and this hurts her somewhat. But she doesn't tolerate fools gladly and describes herself as impatient. She admits to occasions when she has actually thought of giving up everything and going off alone. She has changed quite dramatically since she got married. She feels there are times when her husband must think that she is extremely selfish and maybe he is also a little resentful that she is out so much, but she wouldn't give it up. The most important thing for her now is to see her three children manage to get through to a stage where they're independent. She says she has no huge ambitions for them but would like them to do something that *they* want to do, whatever it is.

One of her regrets is the loss of friends through politics. Very often she finds herself the only woman talking to men at parties and feels women resent that. She feels her public role very often intimidates women and that being seen with male politicians can be misinterpreted as 'being loose'. It's not the kind of thing people think about men, she says. She can also spot the resentment towards her on the part of some of her male colleagues and is aware of their sexist remarks. She has made friends in Leinster House but regards many of the friendships as quite superficial. She socialises with colleagues but wonders what kind of speculation this provokes. She describes Leinster House as a very unfriendly place and feels that being in politics is lonely. 'I'm very conscious that sometimes I'm slightly apart from my friends, although I try not to be. I'm treated differently even walking around doing my shopping.'

It will make a difference to her to have other women deputies in the Dáil, but she feels that each woman will have to fight her corner with her party whip when it comes to getting speaking time and she doesn't see any role for a close grouping of only-women deputies. She says there are times when women have to be pushy and tough. It goes with the job. There are times when she would love to be a shrinking violet; but she's not and she's never going to be.

Róisín Shortall

First elected to Dáil Eireann:
November 1992 — Labour Party

Róisín Shortall, one of Labour's four Dublin women deputies, sees herself as a politician who happens to be a woman rather than as a woman politician. She sees no difference between being a female or a male politician nor does she see herself as particularly promoting the women's agenda. She consciously kept away from the Women's

Committee of the Labour Party, feels strongly that women's issues should be mainstream issues and says there's a serious risk of marginalising them if they are dealt with separately. But she is definitely a socialist and says she is a socialist above all else. To some extent she resented the focus on the twenty women deputies in the first few days of the 27th Dáil. But she does think the new Ministry of Equality is a good idea because minority groups have fallen very far behind, especially the handicapped and travellers.

Róisín comes from a very political family. Her father was a Dublin city councillor for a short while, and one of her brothers stood for election in the 1970s. Her home was regularly used as an election headquarters. But originally it was to Fianna Fáil that the Shortalls gave their allegiance. Róisín didn't join the Labour Party until 1987. She is adamant that she never had any time for Fianna Fáil. There was never anything about the party, she says, which attracted her.

Her father fought on the Republican side in the civil war but supported Fianna Fáil from the day the party was formed in 1926. Her mother became involved in Fianna Fáil when she met her father and she was active for most of her life. Róisín shared the family interest in politics and was fully involved in family arguments and discussions of political issues.

Perhaps it was because she was the youngest in the family and spent a lot of her time with adults that Róisín became what she called 'a rebel' in Dominican College, Eccles Street, Dublin. She had difficulties with the nuns and with what she describes as their 'pettiness and their snobbery in dealing with the less well-off pupils'. She was resentful of this and felt from an early age that the whole system was unfair. This carried over into her not wearing the full school uniform which also got her into trouble. She says she always believed in speaking out in school and she regularly made her views known. She remembers a particular occasion when the head nun asked for a guarantee that the girls would behave. Róisín could only promise that she would *try*. She ended up in the convent parlour and her mother was called in. 'In fairness she stood up for me,' says Róisín. But today her attitude has mellowed considerably and her eldest daughter is now a pupil at the same school. Generally speaking, she says her parents had a *laissez-faire* attitude to child rearing. She frequently stayed up late arguing the toss and then missed school the next day. That, she says, didn't bother her parents.

She agrees that she was 'a little spoiled and over indulged'. Her father had a particularly soft spot for her but she feels that had things been more strict at home she might be a little more disciplined now.

For Róisín Shortall, growing up in Drumcondra on Dublin's northside was a happy time. Her father worked for the Gas Company. Her mother was a dressmaker. She was a self-confident child but rejects any suggestion that she was pushy. However, she does admit to having some problems with authority. At school she felt alone, but puts this down to the fact that she was living with seven adults while her classmates were often the eldest in their family.

Her father was strict about one issue regarding his daughter. She had a boyfriend when she was about twelve but her father put his foot down about her going to Sunday afternoon discos. Strangely enough, she says, she accepted it. Her father worried about them, she says, and always waited up for them if they were late home at night, even when they were well into their twenties. She remembers how he always kissed her mother when he was leaving the house and was more demonstrative with Róisín than with the others, but again, she puts this down to her being the youngest.

Surprisingly Róisín decided she wanted to teach. She sees no contradiction in her rebellious behaviour and choosing teaching as a career. She explains this choice by saying that maybe she thought she could do a better job herself. While her family were impressed by academic achievement there was very little pressure put on her to do well at study and her parents had nothing to do with her choice of career. She wanted to go to a teacher training college but did not have honours Irish. So she took a year off and did some substitute teaching which she enjoyed immensely.

Her guiding principle was, and still is, that the individual *can* make a difference and that it is possible for an individual to influence the course of history and, on a smaller scale, the way people approach life. She wanted to influence the way people think. She decided to go to University College Dublin (UCD) where she did a BA in History, Politics and Economics. But she didn't enjoy what she describes as 'the rarified atmosphere of UCD'; she felt it was cut off from the real world. This is a feeling she has about a lot of establishments. At UCD she felt alienated because she was both a northsider and a loner. No-one from her class in Eccles Street was there and she felt that the connections southsiders could make through schools and rugby clubs didn't apply to her at all. Most of the friends she made were northsiders but she found a lot of the students came from well-to-do families; many would be taking over their father's legal practice. 'Life was all mapped out for them,' she says.

She found a lot of student life quite boring. By her second year she was spending very little time in college but didn't think of giving it up. 'I was very unfocussed at that stage in my life.' Her father was then seriously ill with Parkinson's Disease and she spent a lot of time with him. Her one regret on the day she first entered the Dáil was that he was no longer alive to see her there.

After UCD, Róisín was still interested in teaching and she did a course in Marino College which was designed to get graduates into primary education. She took the first job she was offered which was in the School for the Deaf in Cabra. When she started she knew nothing about teaching the deaf, but she quickly became passionately committed to it. She had a political commitment to primary school education. She felt she could influence people best in their formative years and holds strongly that resources should be concentrated in primary education to correct many of society's imbalances. Deafness is, she feels, one of the worst handicaps of all because it is so isolating. She welcomes the fact that sign language is now acceptable and becoming more widespread and feels it diminishes that feeling of isolation. Prior to this, children were coming through an entirely oral system and ending up at sixteen or seventeen unable to communicate with the world. Róisín was very happy to play a part in this fundamental change in teaching. Her first pupils were mildly deaf children who had been regarded as 'slow learners' in their local schools. As a result they were very far behind in their work. Once these same children had hearing aids fitted they came on in her class in leaps and bounds. This gave her enormous job satisfaction. She became very attached to her pupils, especially the boarders, and is going to miss them and her school very much now that she is in the Dáil.

Throughout her thirty-eight years Róisín Shortall has maintained an interest in politics. Keenly aware of the poverty in Irish society, She has found herself closest to the policies of the Labour Party. When the party left coalition in 1987 she and her husband, Séamus, made a conscious decision to join, he first, she a few months later. Unlike previous occasions in her life, this time she slotted in very easily. Having experienced no difficulty in securing a nomination she was swept on to Dublin Corporation as Labour secured huge gains throughout Dublin city in the local elections of 1991. Party officials and supporters were not surprised when she took a seat for Dublin North West in the general election of 1992.

Although only a short while in Leinster House, she would like to see changes in the style of debate in the Dáil. She finds the heckling and the banter unacceptable and says she is intolerant of it. She hopes to make a major contribution in the debates but is conscious that it will take her a while to find her feet. She would like to observe for a while and makes the point forcefully that she likes to be 'in control' and is not comfortable until she is. 'In a new situation like this I take my time about finding my feet.' She feels very uncomfortable talking about things she's not sure of. She finds Leinster House very friendly. But she says the first thing that strikes her about working there is the need for discipline. 'There's always somebody looking to go for coffee and willing to have a chat and there's always a bit of scandal to be exchanged.'

For Róisín Shortall there is nothing she would like to do other than politics. A second choice, if she had to choose, would be full-time involvement in the community in Ballymun, Dublin, part of her constituency. As a TD she intends to be a key figure in her constituents' lives. She feels she has a very important function to perform as a link between her constituents and officialdom. The level of deprivation in her constituency, she says, makes her very conscious of the role of the media in setting the political agenda. She rarely sees the issues which are important to her constituents represented in the media. There are so many people who just don't count any more in this society, she says.

When Róisín was first elected to Dublin Corporation there were times when she felt that she should be doing something else, something on the ground. She's very heartened by what's happening at grassroots level. Ballymun, she says, is a perfect example. It could have been a completely lost cause, but there is enormous energy and enthusiasm in the community. Ballymun is on the way back. The fact that the Labour Party has doubled its representation in Dáil Eireann has made a big difference to her. It's great to see younger people, Dublin people and particularly northsiders in the Labour Parliamentary Party, she says. It makes the party more representative. She says she wouldn't have much in common politically with the party's older rural TDs and feels the new members are more radical and have their feet much more on the ground. There's a note of caution when she talks about being in cabinet. 'I've no ambition at this stage. At some stage in the future I'd be interested. But Taoiseach? No I've never thought of that.' But she is thinking of what her role will be as a government backbencher. This, she says, will be of great concern within the Labour Backbenchers Committee, who are concerned with maintaining their identity as a distinct entity from government and will be strong in determining the role they will have in policy formation.

'I'll just hold my breath on that and see how it develops,' says Róisín as she finds her feet and takes control of her new-found place in Dáil Eireann.

Helen Keogh

First elected to Dáil Eireann:
November 1992 — Progressive Democrats

For Helen Keogh, winning a seat in the 1992 election for the Progressive Democrats was particularly sweet. She had joined the party very early on and was a prime mover in organising the Dún Laoghaire constituency. She was nominated as the party's front runner in the borough for the 1987 election but then head office added the high profile journalist, Geraldine Kennedy, to the ticket.

Helen was extremely disappointed. She knew this would make the campaign very difficult and that it would be a far greater battle for her. She had never stood in an election before and she had no experience of how to run a campaign. 'Suddenly we were in this maelstrom and we were absolutely flying.' The whole focus was on trying to win the seat. Helen's family motto is 'Take the Hill'. It means don't be diverted, come back for your wounded later. With single-minded determination the party did win a seat. Geraldine Kennedy was elected, but Helen Keogh was just another 'also ran'. It was a shattering experience. She thinks the decision to nominate Geraldine Kennedy for Dún Laoghaire was wrong. She says she now has a far better understanding of why the decision was made, but still thinks it was wrong.

She was pleased for the party, but personally it took her a while to come to terms with it. She cried for a day, she says. She felt very, very hurt and resentful but decided to carry on. However, when Geraldine lost the seat in the 1989 election and withdrew from politics Helen felt it was an awful let down. 'My initial reaction was, "my God, I didn't do that. I stuck it out. I really did." ' But then she thought of all Geraldine had gone through that year. She'd lost a baby and for Helen Keogh nothing could be worse than that. She believes that Geraldine Kennedy made the right decision.

During the Fianna Fáil/Progressive Democrats Coalition, Helen was a senator. It prepared her for the 1992 election. When she finally won her seat she felt a great sense of satisfaction. She had worked so hard, she had smiled for five years and never said one single word against anybody. She kept the internal party battles to herself. When asked how she had coped she says it was not as if she had nothing else, as if politics was her whole life. She had other things to hold on to. She had her family. Essentially Helen believes she has something to offer and that people believe in her. Her supporters never faltered and always believed that she would win through. She also decided to throw some of her energies into the party on a national level. She got elected to the party executive.

Helen Keogh is going through another deep sorrow at the moment. This time it's in her private life. She is now converting her house to accommodate her parents. Both have been extremely ill. Her mother has gone through considerable pain as she has battled arthritis through several operations. Her father had a stroke eighteen months ago and is very disabled. He's now in a nursing home which is extremely well-run. But she just can't leave him sitting in a room and wants her parents to be together. For her, it is terrible to see them both cut down in their early 'seventies when they should be still enjoying life.

Helen is an only daughter and has three brothers. Her father was a senior officer and her older brother is also a soldier, in the Irish army. A first generation Dubliner, she was educated by the Loreto nuns, first in Crumlin and then in Beaufort Rathfarnham. She is extremely close to her family and says that as an only girl a lot of family life revolved around her. Her mother is a very lively, extrovert person and worked as a nurse while the family was growing up. Helen occasionally resented this but it gave her mother more independence and she knew that, like herself, her mother would have been lonely if she had stayed at home. Nonetheless she knew nobody else whose mother worked outside the home as the family was growing up. Her mother also ran the home. Helen's father was posted abroad on a number of occasions. He served in the Congo, was one of the first observers to go to the Lebanon in 1958 and also served in Cyprus. Although very close to both parents she says she was closer to her father. Home was very solid, content and secure. But she does remember challenging her father's ideas, especially in her late teens. She remembers feeling very antagonistic towards him then but feels it was all part of normal growing up.

Her father was very protective and when she went to

dances he collected her. 'To Daddy I was always fourteen,' she recalls. She liked school but found a lot of what she was learning irrelevant. She was bright, did enough to pass exams, but seems to have preferred the hockey pitch. There was a strong sense of independence and perhaps the beginnings of a feminist consciousness in her refusal to do home economics and her insistence on doing science. She didn't want to be seen to be doing 'girls' subjects'.

At home there was a consciousness on the part of both her parents that she should not be lumbered with doing girls' work. For her father it had to do with fairness and equity. Her parents were adamant that she and her brothers should get the same opportunities. Career-wise her father would have liked to see her get into teaching; something permanent and pensionable, something she could go back to, something that would allow her to have her own car. She did this for a while before going into business with her husband, Paddy Hayes, in the commercial information field. Clearly the family expectation was that she would marry. But they also wanted her to be economically independent.

She was shy and quite gauche she says, with just a thin veneer of sophistication, at University College Dublin (UCD). She was intimidated and found the transition from school in Rathfarnham to college an awful experience. She now feels a transition year would have helped her hugely and says that both she and a friend who went with her from school, were really overgrown immature schoolgirls. In her first year she felt lost and was very insecure and unsure of herself. She went to the Literary and Historical Society (L & H) debates and looked on but felt intimidated and didn't want to join in. Intellectually she didn't find herself challenged. 'I just absorbed stuff and threw it back at exam time.' She now regrets that she didn't get more out of it intellectually. Some years later she went back to do a Higher Diploma in Education and got far more out of the time she spent at UCD the second time around.

At home there was an interest in politics, but Helen

didn't know how her parents voted. She suspected her father was Fianna Fáil, but her mother, she said, hedged her bets. Her father, being in the army, did not think it appropriate to have overt political views. Having gone to college at the end of the 'sixties Helen was infused with human rights ideas. One organisation she did join at UCD was Amnesty International. There was a keen sense of public service in her family and this, she feels, influenced her in joining both Amnesty International and the Society of Saint Vincent de Paul. She came from a religious family. Her mother attended mass daily but had very liberal views on issues such as contraception. Helen puts this down to the years her mother spent nursing in maternity units. She remembers how, when she came to marry, her friends were astounded at her liberal attitude to contraception, while her newly wedded peers would have come from families where the attitude towards contraception would clearly have been that it was wrong.

Helen Keogh says she became involved in politics through her experience of being a mother and having two daughters. It was the women's movement which first attracted her. Almost by accident she became involved in the Women's Political Association (WPA). She worked for Monica Barnes (Fine Gael) in the 1982 election but still didn't really want to join a political party. She says she wasn't sure about policies but also didn't know anybody who was a member of a party and had no direct link into politics. She stuck with the WPA and in the mid 'eighties served for two years as its President. In 1985 she met Mary Harney (Progressive Democrats). She says that although she was talking to women in other parties, she had no idea what politics was all about. But she felt the urge to become involved and to get other women involved.

Coinciding with these feelings was the establishment of the Progressive Democrats. She decided to join. The main reason for this choice was her excitement at the establishment of a new party. She felt she couldn't really make a commitment to either Fianna Fáil or Fine Gael.

Also, there was the feeling that if you got involved in something that was just starting you could make more of an impact. Something new and radical, she felt, would have a role for women, with which she would feel comfortable.

Like most other politicians Helen Keogh has little time for activities other than politics. But there are some family things she insists upon. Before she married Paddy, they used to meet in the Hibernian Hotel Grill every Friday for lunch and go out together to dinner every Friday night. They still go out to dinner every Friday night but now their two daughters, Rachel and Aoife, go too. And they do the family shopping together on Saturdays. A number of years ago Helen's husband did a course at Harvard Business School in the USA. His experience there showed him how many older men regret the fact that their children grow up without their fathers knowing them. This clearly is something neither Helen nor Paddy intend to let happen to them. Helen's greatest wish for her two girls is that they will be able to avail of every opportunity to do the things they are capable of doing. 'Whatever the hell it is,' she adds. She wants them to do something with their lives. She doesn't care what it is but she wants to open the door of opportunity for them and she wants them to have a deep sense of responsibility towards others.

Helen enjoys extended family dinners. When she is at dinner with her brothers and close friends she says the decibel level rises and rises. Perhaps this is the only clue to the secret passion that she hides behind her slightly shy exterior. She would love to have been an opera singer, a diva, she confides. She would have loved to have some great musical talent, to have excelled at something musical. 'I suppose it's the smell of the grease paint, the roar of the crowd; maybe politics has an element of this too,' she laughs.

Mary Flaherty

First elected to Dáil Eireann:
June 1981 — Fine Gael

Mary Flaherty is of that rare breed of politician who was appointed a member of government on her first day in the Dáil. She had joined Fine Gael just a year and a half previously and was twenty-eight. But her first memory of taking a public position on a political issue goes back to when she was twelve and argued the toss about the Treaty with a friend who came from a republican background. In spite of that early indication of political interest, it was not until her third overture to the party that she actually joined. She came into Fine Gael on the wave of enthusiasm which greeted Garret FitzGerald's leadership and joined Young Fine Gael when it had 5,000 members. Now, over ten years later, she says it's still her active ambition to be a cabinet minister.

Unlike a number of her other women colleagues Mary Flaherty loved University College Dublin (UCD). She had grown up in Finglas and was one of a handful from her area to go on to third level education. Mary was born and reared in East Finglas, near Finglas village, in what she describes as a modest home in a small terrace of red bricked, owner-occupied houses. Her mother was from Mayo and her father from Kerry. They had both worked in Britain during the war and, she says, she was very much a first generation Dubliner. She went to primary and secondary school in the Holy Faith convent school in Glasnevin and was one of a handful from her school and the Finglas area who went to UCD. While there, most of her friends were northsiders and she had a strong northside identity. She describes going to college as a huge culture shock. She had come from a world where people worked from nine to five, married and lived more or less the same as their parents had. For her, university threw everything open. Everything was possible. 'The conventional idea of the safe, secure, cocoon with its traditional views was challenged.' Her mother, she says, regrets this and in a way feels that university stopped her two daughters from becoming entirely safe, conventional catholic girls.

She decided to join Fine Gael in her first year at UCD. Hundreds were joining up and she remembers the first meeting she attended. Adrian Hardiman (now Senior Counsel) was one of the key figures. She'd come across him before at a schools' quiz where his school, Belvedere, had beaten hers, Holy Faith Convent Glasnevin, by one point. She refers to him and others then in the branch as the Dublin 4 set and says their resonating voices and articulation were intimidating. She didn't go back to a Fine Gael meeting for a number of years.

By then she was teaching but found herself under-occupied and doing all sorts of evening courses from German and cordon bleu cooking to creative dance. She was very impressed with the 1973-1977 Fine Gael/Labour Coalition and points to their record on equality and labour law reforms in particular. She felt it was a government which had tried to change and she was interested in a more modern society. She had thought about socialism and rejected it and Fianna Fáil was unacceptable because of TACA, a fundraising organisation of big businessmen supporters of Fianna Fáil. Fianna Fáil, she felt, had become corrupted by an over-involvement with power. While her father had been a Fine Gael supporter, none of her friends was politically active and her decision to join was entirely her own. She had done some work in the 1973 and 1977 elections but hadn't really enjoyed it. Her first impressions of canvassing are rather blurred now except for one distinct impression of intruding into people's homes and not being made to feel very welcome. From there she moved on to labelling envelopes. Not exactly an auspicious beginning, she argues.

After the 1977 election she attended a meeting in Ballymun addressed by Garret FitzGerald, who had just taken over as leader of Fine Gael. She'd been furious watching the results of the 1977 election as a government with so many talents was decimated. 'Fianna Fáil were back, fine people like Justin Keating and Conor Cruise O'Brien were just gone, wiped out.' She was so angry she just had to become involved. She had a boyfriend at the time who did a lot of travelling. He was home on the Sunday afternoon of the meeting and didn't want her to go. But this time she was determined. She went and she joined Young Fine Gael. The former Cork deputy, Myra Barry, was the chairperson; Mary Flaherty became the secretary. Filled with youthful fervour they decided to survey members of the parliamentary party on their reasons for joining the party. For many the issue was integrity. But Mary remembers one response from a person who is still a member of the Oireachtas. He had joined up because it met on Friday nights after the sodality!

Mary remembers that one of her brothers always said she had aspirations beyond her station. She pictured herself as the heroine of the piece and she never saw any reason why barriers shouldn't be broken down. She wasn't easily intimidated. But she'd certainly never thought of becoming a public representative.

Alexis Fitzgerald was lined up to 'persuade' her to stand for Dublin Corporation. The idea had been mentioned previously by the former Government Press Secretary, Peter Prendergast, but her initial reaction was negative. 'Maybe if I was married and settled. Who knows where I'll be living, I said. Maybe some time in the future but not now.' She met Alexis Fitzgerald at a Young Fine Gael meeting to which all the party's councillors who were opposed to the Wood Quay development (the construction of the Civic Offices on the Viking site at Wood Quay, Dublin) had been invited. After the meeting they went for a drink. He sat in to her car beside her and took out the Dublin Corporation diary. She says she had a 'Ballymagash' (from a popular television programme which satirised politics, especially local politics) attitude to local government. But Alexis told her about the Corporation's work, the Vocational Education Committee, the Eastern Health Board. He convinced her that it would be a worthwhile thing to do. She agreed to run and was elected to Dublin Corporation. She speaks of being highly motivated and the fact that Fine Gael was very exciting at the time. There were two important developments happening within the party at that time, she says. There was the struggle between those who identified with Garret FitzGerald and those who still identified with Liam Cosgrave. This made Ard Fheiseanna (annual party conferences) very exciting. Secondly, there was the fact that the party was winning new seats. It took two seats in the by-elections in Cork. Mary Flaherty says she was very lucky. She was the right person in the right place at the right time.

She doesn't remember her first election count or her feelings as she sat in the Dáil chamber for the first time in 1981. She does remember wearing a grey pin stripe suit and feeling she was going to be as good as any of the men. After the Taoiseach was elected on that first day she went off with her parents and her boyfriend for tea. As she left the House she had no expectations for herself. She returned at five past seven with just under half an hour to go before the new Taoiseach announced his cabinet. She was told that the party whip, Gerry L'Estrange, was looking for her. Mary thought it was a joke and asked what does 'looking for you' mean. She found out quickly that in her case it meant she was being appointed Junior Minister for Poverty at the Department of Health and Social Welfare.

She was overwhelmed. The appointment had come as a complete surprise. She had very little political experience and most of what she had was with Young Fine Gael. There was another problem in that the Minister, Labour's Eileen Desmond, was quite ill at the time. That, she describes, as having been both an advantage and a disadvantage. It meant Mary had to take Question Time in the Dáil on a number of occasions. That was a particular challenge for a total newcomer. But she says she acquitted herself reasonably well. She learned to influence the answers to questions herself rather than just taking what the civil servants presented. Ministers can be bosses and should be bosses, she feels, but they cannot always be bosses unless they put their foot down. She didn't find civil servants hard to deal with, but found she needed to watch their advice. There were particular tensions between the coalition partners at the time, both of whom wanted to be seen as the great reformers in the area of poverty. This spilled over into her department. She feels there was insufficient delegation, to her especially, when it came to making announcements of new measures and she was not allowed to follow through with issues publicly. Labour was very anxious to get the credit for reforms. It was extremely important for them in terms of participating in a coalition of that kind. It made life very frustrating for her.

The coalition government fell within months and Fianna Fáil was returned in early 1982. She regrets not having been left longer in her post. During her time as minister she did get some insight into policy formation and administration, but feels six months was definitely too short. There is one particular event which she remembers with delight. She'd been asked to reply to a debate in the Seanad on a fire in the battered women's hostel in Harcourt Street. She was asked to say that the government couldn't find any money for it. Before agreeing to speak she got on the phone to John Bruton who was Minister for Finance, and she also spoke to Garret FitzGerald, saying she couldn't do it. 'Within two minutes they found the money and I was able to announce; I think it was £50,000.'

Once back in opposition she learned that there had been huge envy at her appointment. Garret FitzGerald had been severely criticized for the lack of geographical spread in his government appointments. When the coalition government was re-elected in November 1982 not only was Mary Flaherty not reappointed but her ministry for poverty was also gone. She had hoped to be reappointed to government. She says she was disappointed and her dignity was hurt but what seems to have hurt her more were the feelings of resentment towards her in her position as a junior minister. She was quite happy with those who said it directly to her face and remembers becoming good friends with the Galway deputy, John Donnellan, after he told her he should have had the job she got. For Mary it was the deputies who smiled to her face but criticised her behind her back that really bothered her.

However, at this point other more important factors were affecting her life. On the first night that Alexis Fitzgerald had spoken to her about standing for Dublin Corporation his proposal was purely political. They had gone out as part of a large group after that. Both had other partners and their circle included George and Myra Bermingham, Gay and Norma Mitchell and Jim and Patsy Mitchell. They were on Dublin Corporation together and socialised a lot. In September 1981 Mary got the phone call which resulted in her first date with Alexis. She was junior minister at the time and he was a senator and Lord Mayor of Dublin. Initially, the media took no notice of them, assuming they were in various places in their individual capacities. It was at the Texaco Awards in January 1982 that the realisation dawned. Initially, the attention was all very positive but subsequently she found it very difficult. For example, when she had jokingly said 'Call me Minister' to a colleague who had asked how to address her she found it written up as an example of her arrogance. The attention put enormous strain on herself and Alexis. It was the personal element which bothered her most and what she saw as misrepresentation and misinterpretation. Every element of her life, even the most trivial, was intruded upon. It took her two or three years to recover from this. When she was not reappointed to government she was relieved at least that the publicity would now diminish.

In the November 1992 election Mary Flaherty was one of those whom many believed would lose her seat. But she held on. The constituency had been changed and the inclusion of a section of middle-class votes from the Glasnevin area undoubtedly helped her. She says that when she first stood for election the fact that her mother was a nurse and midwife and had delivered 2,500 babies in the Finglas area was a great help to her. But there's obviously more to it than that. When Fine Gael was losing all round them in the last general election Mary Flaherty held on and was proposed for the position of Leas Ceann Comhairle of the 27th Dáil. Although supported by all the opposition parties the Fianna Fáil/Labour coalition defeated the proposal.

Liz O'Donnell

First elected to Dáil Eireann:
November 1992 — Progressive Democrats

'I don't think that we should behave like men now that
we're in. I think it's important that we should throw the
ladder down to other women and encourage more women
to come in.' Liz O'Donnell felt a great sense of history on
her first day in the Dáil chamber. She also felt a sense of
privilege and a sense of honour. But she's not bitten by the

political bug people talk about. If she feels she's effective and enjoys it she'll stay, but she has no doubt in her mind that she could also walk away from it after one term. She'd have no qualms about turning around and saying okay what's next? 'It would be a devastating game if it was your whole life,' she says sagely.

That attitude exemplifies Liz O'Donnell's character. A supremely practical person, she's tried her hand at a number of careers but has never been afraid to move on when she felt the time was right. She has worked hard at whatever she's done and seems to have a strong sense of the work ethic. She has moved on without regret; except from her work with theatre impressario Noel Pearson. When he went to America he closed his offices here, ending her job with him. She had been his theatrical office manager for nine months. She cried bitterly, she says. She got on extremely well with him, had great fun in the theatre and describes him as pragmatic and tough, qualities which she herself seems to have in abundance.

Liz was just seventeen when she decided to go to London in 1974. She'd done a secretarial course after her Leaving Cert and got a job with Allied Irish Banks (AIB). No-one in her family had gone on to third level. She wasn't particularly interested in doing so and wasn't pressurised by her family, although two of her teachers had great aspirations for her. Her mother was horrified at the thought of her leaving home so early. But Liz was very excited. She describes that period in the 'seventies in the vanguard of AIB in London. The bank had headquarters but they had very few branches. She found herself in a sub office above a solicitor's office in Croydon. There was just herself, the manager and a bank official. It was very much promotional and development work, not domestic banking. She really enjoyed building up accounts with Irish business people living in London, but once a full branch opened she lost interest. She had no interest in domestic banking. But she had a great time. She really discovered London, but rather than becoming part of the

Irish scene, she made friends with English and West Indians. She went to concerts and discos and spent most of her money on clothes, an activity in which she still has a real interest. She relished the cultural mix in London and became interested in soul music.

It was a very formative time for her and she began to seriously consider what she would do with the rest of her life. She saw no future for her in banking and says that at the time they joined, 'girls' were given a green suit. They were all ushered into supportive roles or accounting, dealing with big ledger machines which she hated. There was nothing innovative or creative in their work and she was bored. At the same time she noticed that men who joined just wore ordinary suits but were immediately dealing with clients, enmeshed in the major business of the bank. There was a route there for them which didn't exist for women. It made her angry, but it also woke her up to the fact that she would have to go after what she wanted, actively.

Liz is absolutely clear and unapologetic about being a feminist. It's not obvious from her where her feminism came from initially but her mother, Carmel, was a woman with a strong sense of her own identity who, in spite of having polio when she was young, played camogie and it was through sport that she met her husband, John, who was Irish national sprint champion for many years and played hurling with Dublin and Limerick. Liz's father was in the army. But after the war he got a job in Guinness's. She grew up on Infirmary Road, Dublin, the second of three children, part of what she describes as the 'Labour Aristocracy'. Her grandmother lived on the same road and she considered herself a real Dubliner. Liz's childhood was dominated by Guinness's, their doctor was the company doctor and she spent a huge amount of her time attending sports meetings, often in Guinness's Athletic Grounds, and going to matches. But when she was eleven the family moved to Limerick. It was promotion for her father but her mother was very unhappy at losing her extended family in

Dublin. For Liz herself it was a mixed blessing. Her school in Dublin, Stanhope Street, was very strong on discipline and Liz wasn't happy there. Her teacher was very strict. Liz wasn't very good at Maths, and felt her talents in language and expression were overlooked. In Limerick at the Silesian Convent she blossomed and formed a friendship with one teacher in particular who subsequently left teaching and became a barrister.

Insubordinate in school, Liz says she found much of the curriculum quite boring. She tended to concentrate on her favourite subjects of Latin, English and Fine Art and did not bother too much about the rest. Irreconcilable differences with the church arose for her early on. She found it difficult to cope with limits on freedom of expression. At home she found support for her dissent. Her parents were liberal, not particularly religious and saw no reason why she should just swallow dogma she could not accept intellectually. They generally took her side when she was in trouble. The family were practising roman catholics and Liz says that in childhood she was devout in a personal rather than an institutional way. Religion is still an issue for her and something which she thinks about. She's glad she was raised with religion and sometimes wonders if her own children are missing out on something because neither she nor her husband follow any organised religious practice. She wonders about the loss of old values such as obedience which she doesn't think children now have. Her own children, she says, question everything and while that's good for them as individuals growing up, it makes parenting difficult! As a parent, she says she's still learning. She is a christian and is reconsidering a number of issues, but says she's had so many differences with the Roman Catholic Church that she would now prefer to worship in the Church of Ireland because of its ethos of individual freedom.

When she became disillusioned with banking in London she decided to come home to go to Trinity College Dublin (TCD). By then she was very business oriented. She was going to study her old favourite, English, but thought that was a bit of an indulgence and that she should be more sensible since she was paying for it herself with some support from her parents. She felt she owed it to her family to do something that was more career-oriented. She thought about law and talked to her old mentor from school, Antonia O'Callaghan, who was then at the Bar. She decided on a law degree. It was very academic but she loved it. Reluctantly, she accepts that she's an intellectual in that she loves the theory of things. It's probably the reason why she feels she'll enjoy committee work in Leinster House more than debate in the chamber. She recalls how she led what she calls 'a double life' in college. For three days of the week she was a student, for the other two she typed letters for the chairperson of the Brooks Watson Group. Money was in short supply as a student living away from home and life was frugal. She began to buy second-hand glamorous clothes. However, she has no regrets that she doesn't have to do that any more and has no guilty feelings about buying clothes when she wants to.

In her work with AIB, Liz had found that she was more interested in the human aspects of law and how the law affects people's lives rather than making money for private clients, even though she knew she would have been good at that. She looked for a way of combining her business experience and law. She ended up in a law firm where she was eventually paid more than she would have been if she had become a solicitor. She was there for a few years. By now she was married and had her first child.

Liz traces her real political development to having children. She saw how from now on her life was going to be different, no longer without limits. She suddenly felt obstructed by her sex and the realisation that having a child was going to change her life utterly. She realised that in spite of how much women's lives had changed, women still had primary responsibility for childcare and she felt this wasn't simply an issue of women's rights but an issue affecting the country's workforce. If a woman isn't facilitated during the short years of childbearing she will be lost to the workforce. Liz took a career break to have her two children. She suffered what she calls massive loneliness, a sense of isolation and a loss of confidence. She was doing work for which she wasn't trained and for the first time she felt that nothing had prepared her for it. All her education had prepared her for the workforce; nothing had prepared her for this. Her situation was aggravated by the fact that her husband Michael, as a barrister on circuit, was away a lot and she was alone much of the time. She lost touch with her friends who were not in the business of childbearing. (She now had two children, Laura and Robert.) Her mother and her aunts were marvellous during this time, she says. Michael too was very supportive but he was getting on with his own agenda, she says matter-of-factly. They had chosen their distinct roles but she was now conscious that her role was very onerous on her personally. She read a notice for a meeting at which Dr Anthony Clare was giving a lecture on the question 'Is women's health on the decline?' and thought, 'God, this is a meeting I have to attend.' She was feeling completely on the decline and wondering if she would ever get her confidence back.

The meeting was organised by the Women's Political Association (WPA). Frances Fitzgerald was in the chair. The meeting was packed. She joined the WPA that night and was very quickly on the executive committee and then was elected vice-chairperson. She met Mary Harney, who suggested that she join the Progressive Democrats. As a member of the WPA she had been constantly talking about the need to get more women into politics. Mary Harney asked her, 'What's wrong with *you*?' This made her think about running. She agreed to run in the 1991 local elections in Rathmines. It was a big risk and basically she was doing the party a favour. Michael McDowell had been the deputy for the area. After much thought he had decided not to contest the local elections, but everyone knew he would want to contest the next general election. Not many people gave Liz O'Donnell a great chance of winning. But she felt confident about it. She lived in the area, had been chairperson of the Parent/Teacher Association in the local school and knew a lot of people. She was elected.

However, when the general election came along just a year and a half later, Liz knew she was facing a big problem. She says she was a victim of her own success. Now she was presented as a threat to Michael McDowell. No-one thought there could be two seats for the party so the question was: who would move? Liz says it was a tetchy situation. She did feel pushed around. She made a pragmatic decision. She saw an opening in Dublin South and accepted a nomination just fourteen days before polling day. She had to start from scratch. She couldn't pull in any of the goodwill she'd built up as a councillor, but she got stuck in, built a team and took back the seat Ann Colley had lost in 1989, having headed the poll in 1987. She bears no grudges and says she and Michael have talked about it many times.

She describes her first day in the Dáil as the third happiest day in her life, after the birth of her two children and Mary Robinson's election. She was terribly pleased for her father, who was in the public gallery with her mother, because he'd had a by-pass operation two years before and had been very ill. They were really proud of her and she felt that for them she'd probably been a late starter, had taken a long time to settle down. She felt really grateful for being able to give them the gift of seeing her go into Leinster House as a TD. Liz says Michael, her husband, has no interest in politics, and in fact is fearful of it, fearful of the time it's going to take from her and the damage it might do her. She sees that as an occupational risk. Certainly, she says, her life has taken a change, one that neither she nor he would have anticipated when they married. He married a person who wasn't interested in politics and, he now wryly remarks in barrister-like humour, for somebody to become a politician all of a sudden is like new grounds for annulment!

Joan Burton

First elected to Dáil Eireann:
November 1992 — Labour Party

The Department of Social Welfare seems ideally suited for Labour junior minister, Joan Burton. It is an area in which Labour could make a very significant long-term impact. She feels passionately about how divided our cities have become. As a working-class kid in Oxmantown Road in Dublin's north city she remembers poverty but doesn't remember the city being as divided as Dublin is today. She recalls that there was a lot of class distinction then, but there was an absence of the feeling of complete hopelessness she finds today in some of the new suburbs. There were few communities then completely blighted with no-one in the family working.

One of the things she would like to do is to empower communities so that they will develop and use their own resources. Joan Burton says she sees herself in some of the young people growing up in parts of her constituency of Dublin West. She sees her mother in a lot of the women there, who are tremendously ambitious for their children, who give a lot of attention to their children's education and are involved in a whole range of community activities. She feels that communities now marginalised by mass unemployment must be brought back into Irish society.

Joan clearly remembers the moment she decided she was going to be a Labour candidate. It was Christmas 1985 and she was staying in a friend's house in Nairobi with her husband Pat and her daughter Aoife. She had driven a jeep over dirt roads for 600 miles from Dar Es Salaam. Late one night they were playing an American truth game. The question arose as to where she might be in ten years time. The question of standing for election came up and Joan made her decision. She had joined the Labour Party in 1973 but had never thought of being a candidate for public office. She was much more interested in policy formation. She had been very active in the party and as a woman had felt under no disadvantage. Joan found that in Dar Es Salaam, although many women wore the veil, divorce was available. It seemed ironic that while women in Ireland were apparently more prosperous they lacked the civil right to divorce, a right which was available in a less developed country. The experience in Africa made her far more objective about the position of women in Ireland. But she came back from Africa feeling very strongly that the Labour Party had no women running for office and that the representation of women in the party was appalling.

She'd gone to Tanzania in 1983, just after the first abortion referendum and was living in Dar Es Salaam where she and her husband were both teaching at the university. It was a predominantly muslim city but Joan felt that the situation of women in Ireland was actually worse than it was there. When she came home she got involved in the women's committee of the Labour Party and when she complained about the position of women in the party she was asked, 'Why don't you run yourself?'

Unlike a number of her colleagues, Joan was politically conscious before she left school and says that by sixth year she was a socialist. She grew up near the cattle market in Dublin in an artisan's dwelling. Her father was an iron moulder in Córas Iompair Eireann (CIE) (the state transport company) in Inchicore, as his father had been before him. Her mother had worked in the printing trade before her marriage and did factory work and cleaning jobs at night to help educate Joan and her younger brother Paul. Her father was a supporter of Seán Lemass and her mother voted Labour. That was the extent of political involvement in her home.

She remembers the lowing of cattle and the sound of sheep as she lay in bed on nights before the market and can still remember people diving for cover as the odd bull broke loose when it was being driven to market along the streets of her neighbourhood. Hers was a traditional Dublin working-class family. Her mother's family had been coopers in Guinness's, Jameson's and Powers distilleries. Her paternal grandmother had died of TB and her father was raised in difficult circumstances by his father. It was a close-knit community of what she calls 'sturdy, self reliant, independent' people. Her father had a seat on his bike and cycled all over the city and into the countryside with Joan. Both her parents had a passionate love of the countryside and, once the sun shone, the family took off. They went fishing, took trips to the sea and the mountains. They had another advantage: as a CIE employee her father was entitled to concessionary travel, so there were lots of day trips down the country and a favourite trip was on the *Enterprise* to Belfast. Joan's memories of this city are of shopping, bright coloured cups and saucers and tall policemen with guns.

Joan was very close to her mother and their relationship was to become very special in her late teens. It was her mother who interested Joan in Brendan Behan and the northern playwright, Sam Thompson. According to Joan she set great store by education. Both her parents had left school at thirteen or fourteen but realised that 'getting on' meant being educated. Her mother felt that life was too short for housework and that there were lots more interesting things to do. She felt that it was very important for girls to have a career as well as getting married. As a result, Joan says she never learned to bake a cake.

Joan was a precocious child. She certainly loved the countryside and was in the girl guides, but her real love was books and ideas. She read voraciously in the Capel Street and Phibsboro libraries and her parents' only real worry about her, it seems, was that she would spend too much time with books and not enough in the fresh air. She went to school with the Sisters of Charity in Stanhope Street. She really enjoyed it. With an academic aptitude, Joan got a huge amount of support from both nuns and lay teachers and this was to play a very central role in her life. She had a number of outstanding teachers in school. Sister Stanislaus (Stan) Kennedy (of Focus Point) was working with a youth group in Joan's area and had a number of projects in which the girls in the school were involved. Joan has a certain amount of ambivalence about that. Sister Stan obviously was a social worker and was appalled at the deprivation she saw in the area. But to Joan those 'deprived' were people she had known and grown up with and were her friends or friends of her family and had never been categorised as poor or deprived or disadvantaged. It was different, she says, to see your own world through an outsider's eyes. It was a socially awakening experience for her. Her feelings about it were political. She felt that if things were wrong it was because there wasn't an equitable division of available resources. She was also aware of the housing emergency in Dublin at the time and the devastation of local areas like North King Street and Queen Street. She had also been reading Dostoevsky, Tolstoy, Sartre and de Beauvoir and so was coming under influences which were clearly radical.

Joan thinks she was probably the first girl from her school to go to university. Her parents' thoughts had been very much directed towards a job in the civil service or the corporation or a librarianship. She applied for all of these. But in her last year at school a new civics teacher arrived, who was Austin Clarke's daughter-in-law, and she suggested that Joan go to university. Joan was taken aback at first, then, very interested, but there simply wasn't the money at home. Mrs Clarke encouraged her to apply for a Dublin Corporation scholarship. She says she would have applied for Trinity except the ban was still in force and 'I have to say the nuns in the school were completely cold on the idea of my going to Trinity.' She also applied to Carysfort College.

Ironically Joan's first job after her Leaving Cert was in the registry section of the Post Office. 'It was a tomb-like area full of millions of files. I was waiting for something to happen. I knew I wasn't going to stay at this.' She spent the summer reading the files of postmen who had had accidents and the details of their various claims! She got a call to teacher training. She says the nuns in Stanhope Street had broken their backs teaching her to knit and to sew and also to sing which was no mean achievement. She went alone to her interview in Carysfort and was the only applicant who did so. She was not dressed up for it. She met a professor of music who asked if she was sure she wanted the place. The nuns in Stanhope Street were absolutely delighted when she got the call. She agonised over it, but felt she couldn't go to Carysfort College; she wouldn't survive in the structure which she felt she saw there from the experience of her interview. Fortunately, she didn't have to — the scholarship for UCD came through.

She hadn't the faintest idea of what to study, how to apply or even where UCD was. It was the porter who told her when she arrived that Arts was probably full and to try Commerce. Joan Burton is today a chartered accountant. On the first day she went in to the huge lecture theatre for the B Comm class, there were several hundred students but only a handful of women. She was greeted with wolf whistles, claps and jeers. Joan says she has never seen so many men concentrated in one place in tiered rows until she came into the Dáil chamber on her first day there. She found the two experiences very similar, although the men, in the Dáil are much more polite.

Joan was hit by a major tragedy while she was at UCD. Her mother got cancer. Joan nursed her devotedly until she died almost two years later. Her mother suffered enormous pain and Joan was devastated by her death and the suffering she went through. Shortly after her mother's death Joan's father remarried. Joan remained at home to look after her brother. She found it extremely difficult to look after Paul and herself and manage a household on a scholarship. She took jobs in the evenings and at weekends.

Two of her unmarried uncles and an aunt were extremely good to her, as were her own friends and the families of Paul's friends. She still remembers the relief of the day when Paul got a scholarship to St Patrick's Training College; at least his fees were taken care of. Today he is the Principal of St Laurence O'Toole's Number 2 School, a special project school in Sherrif Street. They are extremely close and Joan is very proud of him.

Joan doesn't feel resentful about what happened to her. Her overriding emotion throughout was one of devastating loss. She talks of how everyone has to die, although its unfair when someone you love has to die, especially when you feel their life should have a long course to run. It's something which one can only come to terms with over time, she feels. But it gave her a greater sense of the value of life and the quality of life and a strong feeling for people with difficulties in their lives. She emerged from the experience with a deep sense of spirituality, not in the sense of organised religion though. It was, she says, a watershed. 'I came through it in the end; that's all I can say.' At times of course she still wonders at what might have been; on her first day in the Dáil she would have loved her mother to have been there. She was lucky enough to have her father there along with her stepmother with whom Joan has a close relationship.

Personal relationships to Joan Burton are very precious. She is very close to her daughter, Aoife. She had difficulties having a child and Aoife will be her only one. She feels very lucky and very privileged to have one daughter. 'I'm just happy about that. I don't think of what other children I might or might not have had. I've just left it at that.'

Joan has always been regarded as being on the left of the party. I asked her if she would have been disappointed if Dick Spring had not included her in government. She says she discussed that very issue with her husband Pat on the night before her appointment. There had been a lot of speculation about her and a lot of phone calls from family and friends. On balance, she did expect to be appointed on the basis that she has a lot to contribute. But she knew there were a lot of other things to be taken into consideration. As far as possible, she said, she looked on it as Dick Spring's choice.

Eithne FitzGerald

First elected to Dáil Eireann:
November 1992 — Labour Party

In the history of Irish politics only one candidate has managed the unlikely record of having failed to be elected in four general elections, and topping the poll, nationally, on the fifth attempt. That's precisely what Eithne FitzGerald, Labour TD for Dublin South achieved in November 1992. As the realisation dawned on the day of the count that she was going to poll over 17,000 first preference votes, she says it felt unreal. Her four brothers (she's the fifth of eight children) have worked as tallymen for her at election counts. They knew when the boxes were being opened that she would get a quota but everyone was amazed at the final vote. Dublin South is one of the country's most volatile constituencies. It had returned John Horgan, a previous Labour deputy. In 1987 it put Anne Colley of the Progressive Democrats at the top of the poll only to deny her a seat next time round in 1989. That year it elected Roger Garland of the Greens only to reject him in 1992. Along with Dublin South West, where two Labour deputies were elected, Dublin South personified the swing to Labour, the electoral appeal of Dick Spring and the drawing power of strong women candidates.

On top of her electoral achievement Eithne FitzGerald was given the post of Junior Minister in the new office of the Tánaiste. As a Junior Minister in finance she has responsibility for European Community Structural Funds. This alone is a big area of responsibility. She will also liaise with government whip, Noel Dempsey, on the implementation of the Programme and will represent the Tánaiste, Dick Spring, on the Social and Economic Forum proposed in the government programme. In addition, she has the challenge and the difficulty of starting something new, an empty corridor with a department being set up from scratch. It's more difficult, she says, than walking into an established department, such as education, which starts at play-school and ends with adult education and where the structures are already established. But she's terribly excited about it and says it will involve virtually everything she's interested in achieving in politics.

Eithne was due to chair a meeting of Dublin County Council's jobs committee at 10.30 am on the day she got a call from Dick Spring's secretary, asking her to be in his office at one o'clock to see him. There was a lot of press speculation, some indicating that she would be appointed while other commentators felt that by numerous appearances on RTE radio and television she had 'talked herself' out of a job. Eithne's attitude to the speculation was mixed. She says she didn't pay too much attention to it but felt that the speculation about the composition of the government seemed to be crystalising around names in a way that suggested it was not just individual journalists thinking out loud, but that fairly solid information was being given to them. She heard about the establishment of the new office of the Tánaiste on the news.

She listened to the Taoiseach's speech in the Dáil nominating the members of the cabinet, in which he gave a description of what the office of Tánaiste would be and thought, 'God, that is really exciting. If my name were to be on it, it really would be a big, big challenge.' When she arrived in Dick Spring's office the cabinet meeting had over-run and he wasn't there. But Brian O'Shea was, as were Emmet Stagg and Joan Burton. The fifth appointee was Jerry O'Sullivan from Cork North Central who didn't get to Dublin until later.

She left Dick Spring's office with Joan Burton to have tea. Eithne admits to being nervous as they waited, 'I had my good clothes on just in case,' she chuckles. Eventually they were called, one by one, and given their assignments. It was only as they trooped down to the plinth at Leinster House for the photo call that they could ask each other what he or she had got. Her thoughts did stray to her other party colleagues. Out of thirty-three deputies there were only jobs for ten in addition to the party leader. While she felt that what was happening to her was important, she was also aware that other colleagues were not being given jobs. Since then, many of them, especially those who had served the party for years, have said that they were far from pleased with the way in which the choices were made.

Though full of her new position and thinking of her responsibilities, she did of course think of her husband, John, and her three children and wondered what it would mean for her family life. There was also the practical thought of dinner that evening. This one was solved by the family celebrating with dinner in a Chinese restaurant. John was the first person she told. He'd come in to Leinster House but by the time she'd been shown her office he had left. She admits to feeling apprehensive and speaks of coming from 'civilian life' and the speed with which things had happened. After the tensions of the immediate post-election period, when there was so much media attention and the hostility she felt because of the party's talks with Democratic Left, she loved switching off at Christmas, peeling loads of spuds, preparing bits and pieces of things for dinner, having her extended family in and thinking of very ordinary things like what kind of stuffing would she put in the turkey or did she need to boil another kettle for the pudding. Since her appointment she's determined to keep Sundays absolutely private and sacrosanct. 'I think if you work hard six days a week, that's enough.'

The new junior minister was born in Dublin and lived in Glasnevin, the daughter of civil servants. There was a very strong public service ethos in the house, but it was not a political household by any means. Her father, she says, was quite apprehensive about politics. There was almost an assumption at home that the children too would become civil servants, as Eithne did for a number of years. Her grandparents and her aunt lived close by. The Botanic Gardens was her playground and she remembers climbing trees, hiding in the bamboos and playing camogie at school. She was good at school and was particularly happy with the Dominican nuns at Scoil Caitríona in Eccles Street. She remembers the nuns as very strong feminists who encouraged their students to aim high.

Eithne's mother died of cancer when she was eleven. Eithne remembers her childhood response. It hadn't struck her or her sisters or brothers that her mother would not get better. 'At that age you've a very simplistic view, a simplistic faith that if you said enough prayers she'd get better.' The loss of a parent or a child, she thinks, is the most devastating thing that can happen to anybody.

Nothing ever prepares you for it. She now feels she would have liked to have known her mother better, to have found out more about her. When her own children were born she remembers feeling really lonely that her mother wasn't there to share the whole thing. She is very close to her sisters and brothers and they still meet regularly. When any of the four sisters is going through a difficult time they ring each other and say 'SIP' (sisterhood is powerful)! It's a code for 'We're thinking of you.'

Like her colleague Joan Burton she got a scholarship to University College Dublin (UCD). Unlike Joan she joined the university's branch of the Labour Party and became involved in the student politics of the late 'sixties. It was very exciting, the feeling that young people could change the world if only they got involved in it. She was still living at home and remembers how other students were ready to occupy buildings all night while she had to go home and be in by a certain time. Her father was very taken aback by her involvement in radical politics. On one occasion she went up north to take part in one of the first People's Democracy marches in Belfast. There was to be a demonstration and a sit down in Linenhall Street. Eithne expected to be home on time so that her father would be none-the-wiser that she hadn't been in the library. It didn't quite work out that way. There was an unscheduled stop at a pub on the way home and when she arrived in Glasnevin her father was furious with her. As a parent now she can understand why he was so angry and worried. While she clearly felt the buzz of being involved in the vanguard of the civil rights movement at another level, violence *was* about to erupt and it could have been very dangerous.

Eithne says romance blossomed for her over the supply and demand curves of her economics class where she met her husband John. They differ on where precisely they met but she does remember meeting him outside polling stations as they both canvassed for different parties. He is the son of Garret FitzGerald. He was on the Maurice

O'Connell wing of Fine Gael and very opposed to the policies of Finance Minister, Richie Ryan. 'Love,' she says, 'overcame all.' She found her future mother-in-law very formidable, someone she's very fond of now but whom she found initially very intimidating. John himself has found it difficult to deal with the fact that his father has been so much in the public eye. It has been awkward and they've always tried very hard to have their children grow up as anonymously as possible. She has some worries for her own thirteen-year-old daughter and how she'll be affected by her mother's new public role.

For years Eithne has been going in and out of Leinster House doing background work for the Labour Party. She describes the whole security system of having to be escorted through the House and getting a visitor's badge as a pain in the neck. To walk in by herself now she describes as a delight and she says, 'I'm a deputy.' She made her maiden speech on her second day in the House and was very happy to have her father and her step-mother in the public gallery and to see how thrilled they were.

Eithne FitzGerald would dearly love to be Minister for Finance. It's the department she worked in herself when she was a civil servant. She thinks it's very important that women make a mark, not only in areas which are seen as the traditional caring ones. She's convinced that it's harder for women to make it into the Dáil and feels that by and large the women who do so are of an extremely high calibre. She feels it's very important to have a woman in a job that is a serious economic job, just as it was to have had Máire Geoghegan-Quinn as Minister for European Affairs. It's important to show that women can do the serious and tough economic jobs too.

Síle de Valera

First elected to Dáil Eireann:
June 1977 — Fianna Fáil

Although she says politics is her first love, Síle de Valera
speaks passionately about ballet. One of the first people to
buy tickets for the performances at the Point Depot in
Dublin of the great Kirov and Bolshoi Ballets some years
back, Síle still has total recall of the pictures of dancers she
was given in a book as a child. One of her life's ambitions

is to see the Kirov perform in St Petersburg. She speaks of the grace and beauty of the dance and the feat of athleticism it represents for her, a thing of real beauty. She saw her first ballet performance when she was fifteen and later as a student went to performances at the Paris Opera House where she sat in the 'gods'. The recent death of Nureyev saddened her and she speaks of his wonderful interpretive skills – a great technician and a great artist.

Síle de Valera is a shy woman. She finds it hard to enter a large room where she knows very few people. She has also suffered more than most politicians from being stereotyped and has found that much of the media coverage she's received has concentrated on some of the speeches she's made in very specific areas. She's quite happy to be a backbencher. She would like to be a junior minister, but expresses no other great ambition. If she got the opportunity of serving as a junior minister and found she had the ability for it she would then think of a place in cabinet. But, she knows, these decisions would not be hers.

In many respects she's a traditional TD. She has reconciled the question of conflict between constituency work and legislative work. She doesn't feel that clinic work and what she calls the 'messenger boy politics' holds back legislative work. While it does take up a lot of time she believes that it's extremely important to keep one's feet on the ground and to understand the problems of people not just from a theoretical perspective but from a real and practical point of view.

As a woman TD a lot of women come to see her, just to talk. They see her as having a sympathetic ear and as someone who will protect their privacy. They discuss issues which, she says, are much more psychological than political and they do so without embarrassment. They are far less inclined to approach male TDs in this way.

Síle de Valera became a psychologist after she was elected to Dáil Eireann and feels that her training helps in her work. She refutes the suggestion that it's because of the lack of other services that people with personal difficulties come to TDs to talk about them. She believes it's because in small communities people often have difficulties in coming to terms with *the very fact* of having problems and requiring help, and some see this as an admission of failure on their part. However, once it comes to political issues she doesn't think constituents differentiate between male and female TDs. They're looking for commitment, availability and ability to deal with issues. She thinks that women politicians have a different approach to men on many issues and that strong representation of both sexes gives a more rounded view of the world generally. She has a very positive view of the work done by the Oireachtas Women's Committee, of which she was a member. There was no real sense of party politics there, she says, but a practical approach to getting things done. She feels this was achieved because most of the committee's members were women who had a different approach. Theirs was a sense of connectedness, a sense of community and a sense of the practical application of how their decisions would affect people. Much more business was done in the committee as a result, she feels. When it comes to whether or not she defines herself as a feminist, Síle is thoughtful. If feminism means positive discrimination and women being placed in positions at the expense of men, then she is not a feminist. If it means that women have the same equal right to participate in any kind of work they wish; have equal rights to educational opportunities, that's a different matter. She believes that if there is real gender equality in education, attitudes will change and there will be change in the whole system.

Síle joined her local Fianna Fáil Cumann (branch) in Cabinteely, Co. Dublin, when she was seventeen. She was elected to Dáil Eireann in 1977 at the age of twenty-two. Looking back on it, she says it may have been a bit daft, she was so young, but political opportunity doesn't always present itself at the right time. When she joined the party she was studying History, Politics and Philosophy at University College Dublin (UCD). She wanted to see the practical application of politics and says she didn't automatically join Fianna Fáil but looked at the other parties and ultimately felt most at home there. She was attracted not only by the party's tradition but by what she calls its firm policies on how the country should develop. She had no specific ambition to run for office when she joined the party, and accepts that it's been difficult to carve out her own identity as a person, as distinct from being a member of a very famous family.

A well-known name on a ballot paper was certainly an advantage to her, but otherwise it was extremely difficult to set aside the name and forge her own particular identity as a person, both privately and politically, and to establish her own personal worth. People, she says, judged her from a political point of view, whether she wanted to be judged that way or not. She feels there is no point in being resentful of this but she does feel frustrated and wishes people would judge her by what they see rather than by the baggage that is associated with her name. It's not that she's not proud of her family, but she would like to be seen as her own person. Her experience as a public de Valera has made her wary and she struggles to protect whatever privacy she can.

She lives alone in Ennis and loves it. Although she grew up in Dublin she welcomed the change to a small town. She likes the fact that in rural Ireland there's time for people and time to talk. She likes to talk, to get to know people. She had some friends when she first moved to Clare but has made a lot more. She loves the music of Clare, the sense of history that she finds in the people, and she loves to attend the local drama festivals in the county. Belonging to a place is very important to her and she feels she belongs in Clare. She makes time to read and she enjoys cooking for gatherings of friends. It's something she'd love to do more of if she had the time. Pâtes and soups are among the things she enjoys making and she admits that she has a very sweet tooth.

When personal remarks were made about Síle de

Valera's weight on a satirical radio show some years ago she found them very hurtful. She notes that remarks of this kind are more frequently made about women than about men and says it shows a very regressive view. 'They shouldn't be made about men either,' says Síle and she feels a very delicate line should be drawn between people's personal and professional lives. That line, she says, is not always recognised and she feels it is quite unprofessional of the media/commentators to cross it. Apart from her own reactions she found the reactions of people whom she just vaguely knew very interesting. They were absolutely irate, as were some politicians outside her own party who made their views known to her. The question of her weight has no bearing whatsoever on how she does her job or on who she is and what she is.

This question of who she is and what she is has a particular importance in Síle de Valera's case. Her father Terry refused requests to stand for the Dáil and had no professional interest in politics. He wanted a very private lifestyle. Síle says he often jokes that he is the forgotten generation: he's always referred to either as his father's son or his daughter's father, never as himself.

Síle's immediate family is small, just one sister Jane, but she says they are very close. Síle was twenty when her grandfather, Eamon de Valera, died, so she knew him very well and spent a lot of her childhood Sundays in Aras an Uachtaráin. She says her grandmother, Sinéad de Valera, was really the stronger of the two. It was she who had to keep the family together when her husband was on the run, in prison, or involved in political activities. She greatly influenced her husband, not just in his interest in the language, since they met through the Gaelic League, but in her republican views. She was the daughter of a fenian and came from a revolutionary tradition. She was an extremely strong woman who was known by her sisters and other family members as 'Ruthless Aunty Jenny'. She was fiery and not the quiet person that people perceived her to be. But for her grandchildren she was the person they went to with their troubles. Síle feels that Sinéad would have preferred not to have been in public life and she would have preferred her husband not to run for the presidency. She was a family-type person, who would have liked to have maintained her privacy and to have brought up her family and lived her own life in private.

For Síle her grandfather was also very much a family man although the public perception of him was quite different. He would be first on the phone at exam time to wish her luck or congratulate her. Perhaps this was not surprising, since he'd been a teacher himself. He knew she was interested in politics, encouraged her interest and never fobbed her off with pat answers. She says she never felt under his shadow when she went into politics. She shared very many of the fundamental views he expressed but never felt she'd been 'handed on a baton'; rather, it was her own interest in political matters that she wished to express and this has been her driving force.

Síle loves to travel. Her favourite cities are Paris and Florence. She loves the sense of history she finds there, the wonderful architecture. As a member of the European Parliament, where she served for five years, she was in Sri Lanka when the Tamils and Singhalese were locked in conflict. She was also part of a European Parliament delegation which went to Naples to investigate the distribution of community funds for housing and the allegation that the Mafia was getting its hands on the money. But one of her most shocking political experiences was last year when she visited Rio de Janeiro for the Earth Summit. The differences between rich and poor and the grinding poverty of the millions in the favellas, she says, really depressed her. The way in which priests working in the favellas confronted problems, including the drug barons who tried to infiltrate their communities, could teach us some lessons in dealing with poverty in Ireland.

For Síle de Valera, Leinster House is not an easy place to be in. She talks of the debilitating nature of twelve-hour days. The system, she says, creates a very false atmosphere. Firstly, one is dealing with political parties. TDs obviously accept and espouse the views of their own particular party, but in some ways because of those enforced groupings many feel it impossible to cross party boundaries in terms of friendship. For her that's a very unwise attitude. She has made very close friends in other parties. Independence of thought for her enriches a friendship, breaking down political barriers and prejudices. As a result she has made bonds that she hopes will last for life.

Theresa Ahearn

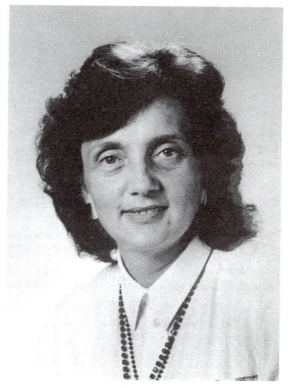

First elected to Dáil Eireann:
June 1989 — Fine Gael

'I just couldn't describe to you the loneliness of being in Leinster House when I came here first. The isolation. You'd have to experience it to understand it. One of the main difficulties is finding out what the place is all about. You just have to learn by yourself.' Theresa Ahearn was on South Tipperary County Council for six years before being elected a Fine Gael TD in 1989. She had fought every inch of the way to become a public representative, but nothing had prepared her for Leinster House and she found little friendship when she arrived. It took her eighteen months to overcome that unease and to be comfortable in the House. It was a deep shock to her to discover she had to find out everything for herself. She wanted to be an active TD. She wanted to participate in the Dáil and not just deal with representations from groups, although she enjoys that. She wanted to be involved, to make an impression. She says she's probably impatient in that she wants to learn everything immediately. She found out the hard way that you have to learn by experience and a crucial aspect of that experience is learning to wait.

Nothing in her family background or her experience growing up had prepared her for the Dáil. She is the youngest of three boys and three girls, born near Golden in Co. Tipperary on what she calls 'a good family farm' of over one hundred acres. Her mother, Catherine, was forty-eight when she was born, her father, John Scott, over fifty. They were totally committed to Fine Gael and both had been Blueshirts. Their next-door neighbour was a Fine Gael councillor and all Theresa's family supported Fine Gael. She remembers the dominant topic of conversation when she visited relatives was usually the vexed question of when Fine Gael was going to get back into government. When she was a student in Dublin the train ticket would arrive at election time enabling her to go home to vote for Fine Gael. Even today her family's politics haven't changed and most of them are still party members.

With her family Theresa worked on the farm, milked cows and fed calves. There were long bicycle rides in the country and outings to football or hurling matches; the family were strong Gaelic Athletic Association (GAA) supporters; she was a member of the Pioneer Total Abstinence Association, and the family rosary was said at home each night. Church-going was a very important aspect of family life. Her father was a deeply religious man and very generous. She can never remember being short of pocket money. Theirs was a rural family which had lived in the area for generations. She didn't even have a cousin in the town and often wondered, growing up, what town houses were like. She knew little about poverty and says she was tremendously secure. Her parents never went out at night and she never remembers a family argument. She grew up in the 'fifties and early 'sixties. If there was any drawback in growing up during those times it was that her youth, like others of her time, was totally unquestioning.

Theresa describes her mother as very liberated and says she had a fantastic influence on her. She was determined that her daughters would have a career, that they would always be independent and retain their jobs when they got married. She had strong ideas that women should only have the number of children they could cope with. She was perhaps influenced by the fact that her own mother (Theresa's grandmother) died in childbirth. The youngest of six children herself, there were just eleven months between each of the six, and her father died eleven months after her mother. All six were reared by an elderly uncle and aunt but she never had the joy of having her mother around and she constantly reminded her own children of that. She loved to sing and recite poetry. She'd finished secondary school herself but stayed at home on the farm until she married. The dominant spirit in the Ahearn household was egalitarianism and everyone was expected to be part of the team.

Growing up, Theresa wanted be a school teacher. She also wanted to marry a farmer. She thought she'd have a family and never wanted to remain single. She saw herself having a career outside the home and never questioned but that this would happen. She loves rural life and loves small rural communities. She certainly never foresaw herself in politics but was always involved in something and says that when she joined any club she wasn't just a member, she would inevitably end up organising people and events. She went to University College Dublin (UCD) with her best friend, Joan Landers. They'd been friends since primary school. She stayed in a flat with her two sisters who were nurses. She felt no insecurity in Dublin. She went from one totally secure situation to another. However, although she loved college, she regrets not having utilised it to the extent that she could have. She didn't join many societies and apart from one friend from Dublin all her friends were from the country. She admits to having had an inferiority complex coming from rural Ireland to UCD but also says that college life did nothing to involve her. She's convinced now that she missed out on a lot. In the summer holidays her father didn't approve of students going off to do factory work and Theresa went home and helped on the farm. She also regrets not having gone abroad to teach for a short while after she qualified with a BA in History, Economics and Maths.

She taught briefly in Navan while doing her Higher Diploma in Education in Maynooth. She had a good time but found teaching difficult in the early years. She was very idealistic and expected a lot of her students. She was a strict teacher and also, as the only young, new, teacher in her school, didn't find her colleagues particularly stimulating. Conversation at lunch time tended to be about marriage, babies, new houses and furniture, things in which she had little interest. She returned to Tipperary to teach maths at the Central Technical Institute in Clonmel. She was there until the day she was elected to Dáil Eireann.

Theresa Ahearn would probably never have persisted in fighting for a nomination if it hadn't been for her husband, Liam. When the going got really rough in Fine Gael it was he who encouraged her. 'He was absolutely brilliant. Fantastic. He gave me every bit of encouragement and would not hear of me pulling out. He was determined I was good enough to make it and as good as any of the other candidates.'

Theresa and Liam met at a Macra na Feirme debate in December 1973 in the local hall in Bansha. The motion was

'Ireland should forget its past.' Theresa had joined Macra partly because she enjoyed debate. She loved everything about the organisation. It had a great social aspects to it with lots of drama and singing and a educational basis. The organisation did things properly. Meetings were correctly held. People spoke through the chair, they proposed and seconded motions. It was a great training for politics.

Theresa liked her future husband even before he asked her out. 'He's a fine looking man, tall, dark and handsome, very quiet and very sincere,'she says. He is eight years older, and at thirty-one, he seemed very mature and she felt very secure with him. She loved dancing. He had no interest in music, 'he'd hardly recognise Sliabh na mBan,' but they came from the same background. He farmed about twenty miles from her family home. They married three years after they met.

Once married, membership of Macra was no longer really appropriate. It was primarily for single people. Theresa says she found its absence left a void in her life. She was still teaching but had nothing to do in the evenings and had always felt that both she and her husband should have an interest in something other than his farming and her teaching. She considered joining the Chamber of Commerce but opted instead for Fine Gael. Apart from her family background, Garret FitzGerald had been one of her tutors at UCD and had a strong influence on her. She wrote to him but it was a year later before she ended up in her local branch. She attended her first meeting in Grange local hall in 1979. 'I can still see the amazement on their faces when I walked in.' She was the only woman and says she didn't see another woman at a meeting for two years. She was drawn into the organisation. On the second night she became secretary of the district council, then constituency secretary and after a chat with the Fine Gael handler, Peter Prendergast, she became Fine Gael's first woman organiser. She was director of elections in South Tipperary in 1981 and for the two elections of 1982. She was then elected to the national executive, but this was her first taste of opposition. She had to fight for a nomination. In 1983 her local councillor died. 'For the first time I indicated that I would like a co-option. I saw a very different side to my welcome to politics. All of a sudden from being a good secretary and a good director of elections you were being asked very indirectly, "Well, is public life for you? Your children are very young." ' She won the co-option by one vote. Theresa Ahearn says that she felt she was not wanted and so she rose to the challenge. Three women had a vote at the meeting but she couldn't get one of them to vote for her. She still can't understand why she didn't get one of those three votes. In 1983 she says there just wasn't the realisation of the importance of a gender balance in politics. Mary Robinson's election has changed all that.

That battle for co-option was the first experience in her life of feeling unwanted. By that time she was just thirty. She had held office at every level in the organisation and felt there was nothing else for her to do but go for national office. The one thing that might have deterred her, she says, was the low regard in which politicians were held. She hated the thought of being tarred with that brush. She didn't like her name being the topic of public conversation. That was the hardest part of it.

Today she would have no difficulty advising her children to go into politics. For her it's a very hard life but an interesting one. Initially she didn't like the idea of being away from home two nights a week. She decided that whatever extra money she had would go into looking after her family. But there were aspects of her home life which made her life as a TD easier. Her mother-in-law lives in her own section of their house. Liam is at home and a very good woman comes in every day until eight in the evening to help her out. She misses her family while she's in Dublin but says it's now part of her life.

She doesn't socialise in Dublin and very rarely visits the Dáil bar. She stays with her sister and never leaves the Dáil before ten or ten thirty at night. She regards Tuesdays through Thursdays as being work days and does a lot of her constituency work from her Dáil office.

When Theresa Ahearn first came to the Dáil she found very little support or friendship from her women colleagues. She says it wasn't that they denied it and adds that perhaps she should have gone looking for it. Whichever, it wasn't on offer, except from Madeleine Taylor-Quinn, who was helpful to her. She found this lack of support amazing and says that the friends she's made were all the people who were elected with her and they were all men. The women in Fine Gael at that time had been elected some years before her. She's very committed to equality issues but never wanted to concentrate on them. She says that there was no-one better than Nuala Fennell and Monica Barnes to fill that area. She genuinely feels that both women are a great loss to the Dáil and particularly admires what she describes as Monica Barnes' 'deep passion'. But Theresa always questioned why women's issues should be totally identified with these two women. She herself was a young married woman with a young family, she was a woman from rural Ireland and yet when any programme was being done on women's issues she was the last to be called, although she feels her life was closer to the ordinary woman than some. It's something she resents.

If Theresa Ahearn has a way of indulging herself, it's in buying clothes. She loves fashion and says she spends 'too much' on clothes. But then, she works hard, she doesn't drink and does very little socialising. As a public representative she's conscious that those she represents, especially women, like her to look well. She feels she owes it to them.

Theresa Ahearn says her time in politics has been tough but she remains undaunted. She admits that in the past she might have been naïve. She worried a lot if she thought things weren't working out right for her. But she remains adamant about one important point. Unlike her experience at local politics Theresa insists that in Dáil Eireann she has never found any attitudes which would belie a mentality encouraging inequality.

Máirín Quill

First elected to Dáil Eireann:
February 1987 — Progressive Democrats

For Máirín Quill, TD for Cork North Central, leaving
Fianna Fáil to join the Progressive Democrats was in a
sense like eating part of her own flesh. Both her parents
were founder members of Fianna Fáil; her father had
fought in the War of Independence and the Civil War. Her
home in South Kerry was headquarters for the republican

side in the Civil War. Erskine Childers (junior) had sat with her grandfather at the family fireside. Liam Lynch stayed in the house three days before he was killed in the Knockmealdown Mountains. Her family were ardent nationalists and she says she was breastfed on politics.

She was the third of six children, with one older brother and sister and three younger brothers one of whom died tragically at thirty-seven. Máirín, who is single, is extremely close to her one sister Ita, with whom she owns a nineteenth-century house in Cork. She has lived there since she rented a flat in it as a student. An avid reader, she has a library of more than one thousand books and always reads herself to sleep. Last year she re-read all of D. H. Lawrence whom she hadn't read for years. She reads on the train and there's always a book on her desk, often a book of poetry. She says her one weakness, or indulgence, is clothes. She inherited this trait from her mother who was always well dressed, always had the best hat in the parish and always wore it well. Máirín never dressed down for school when she was teaching, or up for mass, and her former pupils remark, when she meets them, on how they loved her colourful clothes and the way she dressed for school as if even then she was going to parliament. She buys classic clothes and they last her a long time. Her current winter coat is on its seventh year.

Three men have greatly influenced Máirín Quill's life, and her association with them, in a way, marks three epochs in her life. The first was her father whom she describes as witty and happy, a great man for singing a song, a man who could sing better than most. She related more to him than to her mother and says she doesn't have many of her mother's characteristics. Her mother was a great home maker, she knitted all the family's sweaters and socks; she was a great woman with her embroidery and her needle. The Quills had piped water before others in their South Kerry village because her father was the curator of the local reservoir which was on their land. That set them slightly apart since her mother didn't have to go to the well. Her grandfather, a Parnellite, was chairman of the Kenmare Board of Guardians which built the cottage hospital in Kenmare. Many of her father's friends were from the days of the Civil War, but Máirín's mother was also very interested in politics. 'She was shoulder to shoulder with my father in discussing politics. They were a good pair.' There was no doubt about the Quill's sense of identity.

They were passionate people, says Máirín, with a very strong sense of social justice. One of her father's brothers went to America after the Civil War and became a founder member of the Transport Workers' Union there. Máirín feels he took his sense of struggle for social justice with him. She knew him growing up; he came home on frequent visits, and she was aware of his importance. She feels he too may have influenced her and fuelled her interest in politics.

Like so many other Irish families, especially those who were comfortable, Máirín's parents saw education as the one thing they could give their children. They were all sent away to school and at twelve Máirín left for boarding school in the Presentation Convent in Mountmellick. She speaks with a great sense of poignancy about her days there. She says it was an appalling experience and she feels she shouldn't have been sent. It had nothing to do with the school itself. She enjoyed the academic part, had very good teachers and was extremely conscious that she had no option. The alternative was to take the boat to England, which is what every other girl in her primary school class did. 'I found it terribly difficult to be wrenched away from my family and to be transplanted to a place which, emotionally, was as far away as Afghanistan. I'll always remember the first morning getting up and seeing the flat, dull midlands. There wasn't a sign of a mountain. I thought it was an extraordinary place.' Her feelings never changed about school and she found boarding-school life very artificial. She was consumed with loneliness, even though her sister was there and she'd had cousins there previously. Looking back she says she probably wasn't any more lonely than anyone else. It was the system, and life in boarding school is lonely for everyone. There was a long history of teaching in her father's family and it seemed inevitable that she and her sister would follow the same course. Máirín Quill got a job teaching in Cork. She loved it and did it for all her adult life, until she became a full-time politician in 1987.

She joined Fianna Fáil, or, as she still refers to it, 'the organisation' in Cork in the 'sixties. She had no idea of becoming a public representative but says it was the natural thing to promote the party. She was reared with that sort of ethic. Her father thought de Valera was next to Almighty God. Those influences, she says, are very strong and they were there from a very early age. 'I think my joining Fianna Fáil was inevitable,' she says. A number of things militated against her thinking of herself as a public representative. Firstly, any of the previous women elected in Cork had political family names, Mary McSweeney, (sister of Terence), Myra Barry (whose father was the Fine Gael TD), Eileen Desmond (widow of Labour TD). Máirín says they were all distiguished women in their own right, but they carried into an election situation the advantage of a well-known name. There was also the view within the party that the women were there to do certain aspects of the work, make the sandwiches and the tea. Máirín was a Cumann secretary for years and did a lot of organisational work.

She describes those years as a time of enormous optimism. Fianna Fáil held three of the five seats in Cork city. She remembers, 'with extraordinary pleasure', Jack Lynch's arrival home after being made Taoiseach in November of 1966. 'All of Cork just came alive. There wasn't a house that hadn't people standing at the door or looking out the window.' Cork was alive with excitement, with delight and with pride. She rejects any suggestion of triumphalism. Hurling was like a religion. Jack Lynch was a hurler and footballer of exceptional ability and he had done them proud. He is the second man who has greatly influenced her life.

In the 1977 general election Máirín Quill was one of what she calls the 'infamous group' of candidates who were added by the party leadership to locally selected candidates. Jack Lynch asked her to stand on the basis that he wanted to bring new blood into the party. To everyone's amazement she polled very well. It was a great asset to her in one sense, but a great drawback in another. All hell broke loose following the imposition of candidates especially among city councillors in Cork, who felt they had made the running for the party and were half way to a Dáil seat. Instead of campaigning for her, she says they were actively campaigning against her. It was a baptism of fire. In 1979 the sitting Labour TD, Pat Kerrigan, died. Once more Jack Lynch wanted Máirín Quill to run in the by-election. But, she says, it was made certain that she wouldn't get through the selection convention. On the first vote she got forty votes; six votes later she had thirty-nine. Not only did she not get a single transfer from those eliminated, she actually lost one of her original votes. She did, however, contest the local elections in 1979 and took a seat on the city council.

Máirín Quill's first doubts about Fianna Fáil came from her father's attitude to TACA, the party's fundraising organisation. She remembers him telling a TD 'if you must have TACA type support keep them in the bandwagon but don't let them do the driving.' She would have preferred big business and politicians to have kept a healthy distance from one another. She was also unhappy with Fianna Fáil's role in a number of planning decisions and her experience in the selection conference for the 1979 by-election was a sorry one. She became further disenchanted with the party's handling of Northern Ireland and felt successive governments ought to have matured enough to confront the situation and sit down as equal partners with the British in resolving it. So, when Des O'Malley came to Cork in August 1985 and told her he was thinking of forming a new party, she was ripe for recruitment. She told him it was time for a party like the Progressive Democrats and that she would help him build it. She admires his attitude to the North and says he has great political intelligence, integrity and courage. After her father, who died in 1966, and Jack Lynch, Des O'Malley was the third great political influence on her life.

Perhaps all of these events explain why Máirín Quill felt so triumphant when she took her Dáil seat in 1987. Winning the seat was 'absolutely fantastic, it was really, really fantastic,' she says. No-one had predicted she would ever win a seat. People in Fianna Fáil never gave her a prayer. 'I'm humble enough to admit that it gave me great personal satisfaction to prove the lot of them wrong.' For her first two or three days in the Dáil she found it hard to convince herself that she was part of it. She kept behaving as if she was just a spectator. She spent hours in the chamber listening to debate. It took her a while to convince herself that she wasn't a spectator. She says she didn't have time to feel intimidated by the place because at her first parliamentary party meeting she had to get to know her new colleagues. Michael McDowell she describes as miles, aeons, away from anything she ever knew or experienced. Within two days she'd made her maiden speech on a private members' bill, The Woodlands Bill, dealing with the Coolattin Woods.

Like almost every other new TD, Máirín Quill found Leinster House a most user un-friendly place. She didn't know where to sit in the chamber on her first day. 'But there's nobody to hold your hand. Everybody in politics has to make her or his own way.' Máirín stays in Buswell's Hotel when she's in Dublin, which is at least two nights a week. She describes locking her door at night as a very unreal experience. 'If you find yourself without a book, for example, you're in a panic; it's unlike being at home, where if you wake up in the middle of the night you can just wander into the next room. It's a very lean life.' Basic needs are looked after but there's no extra comfort. Buswell's is a family-run hotel and the staff are extremely helpful and friendly, but it's still a hotel. Máirín Quill misses her garden terribly, although she admits she now has very little time for it. But more than anything else she misses her friends and having time to be with them. Not having time for friends, she says, is the greatest price one pays for being in politics. She finds it an extremely difficult life. The whole political culture is really a male culture. 'What do the men do when there are late sittings? They go to the Dáil bar. But what else can they do?' Máirín Quill doesn't find the Dáil bar intimidating, but says to wander into any bar alone doesn't come naturally to her. It goes against the grain. There's no great social life attached to politics, she says.

Politics has taken up an enormous amount of Máirín Quill's life. But she doesn't feel that being unmarried has anything to do with her being in political life. She has met a lot of men in politics and has access to a broader range of men than one would, for example, in a swimming club. But she does think that, if she had been married and had children, she would not have been able to win and then hold her seat. She has had to give an enormous amount of work to politics. She doesn't regret going into politics and at fifty-two she feels she's learnt a lot about life. When people see her on television they think she has a great life through her involvement. But essentially it's a lonely occupation and particularly lonely for women. She was elected at an age when a lot of other women would be taking up bridge or golf. As a result she has developed parts of her personality which were latent. She's glad that she's had to push back her own boundaries, to hold her own with nineteen men in Cork, to go into a very male situation and not compromise herself in any way. After last November's election the Fine Gael deputy, Peter Barry, described Máirín Quill as 'a politician of backbone'. That meant a lot to her and she hopes she deserves it.

Avril Doyle

First elected to Dáil Eireann:
November 1992 — Fine Gael

The Wexford TD, Avril Doyle, was first elected to Dáil
Eireann in 1982, lost her seat in 1989, won a seat in the
Senate, and was re-elected to the Dáil last November. 'I've
always politically traded under Doyle,' she says, referring
to her marriage name. 'They took me as I was, not who
they thought I might be,' she says, referring to the

117

electorate. She is in fact the third generation of the Belton family to serve in the Oireachtas and describes politics as an all-embracing disease. She says she's a rebel with a cause, and she is quick to point out that she has always been rebellious, but that this trait is now more controlled and focussed. She believes that controlled aggression and properly focussed assertiveness is actually a great weapon. Men think it's their preserve, she says, but she asks why shouldn't a woman be forceful and assertive if she has a passion about something and has a vision that she's single-mindedly pursuing? Men don't like this, says Avril Doyle, because it doesn't fit the stereotype of the convent-educated submissive woman! 'If that's what they're expecting they're on a wrong one here,' she says. 'I was never good at being told what to do. I was always suspicious of authority. My back would be up easily and, if I was told to do something, I probably wouldn't; if I was asked or shown good reason, I might.'

Avril Doyle could be the first woman to lead an Irish political party. Ironically, if she was to replace John Bruton as leader of Fine Gael, as some suggest she might, she would be replacing a former boyfriend. John Bruton and Avril Doyle went out together for two years when she was in her last year at school and first year in University College Dublin (UCD). At sixteen or seventeen, she says, you think it's forever. At the time they were serious. For some years afterwards, she says, there was a slight strain between them but she likes to think that they are now friends, at least to the extent that they can be frank and honest with each other and feel comfortable discussing issues.

John Bruton wasn't her only boyfriend. There were lots of men in her life, but just three months after she graduated with an honours degree in biochemistry, she married Fred Doyle, twelve years her senior, a man whom she'd met at a rugby match in Wexford just eleven months previously. Three years later she was the mother of two daughters and immersed in domesticity. She had joined the local branch of Fine Gael when she moved to Wexford in 1972 and in 1974 she was elected to both Wexford Corporation and County Council. It was the era of Garret FitzGerald; the party was looking for young people and more women in politics. Avril says she was just in the right place at the right time.

Avril Doyle has a huge interest in agriculture and loves the land. Although considered by many the quintessential urban type, she was actually born and grew up on a farm, Belvue Park in Killiney, Co. Dublin. The land today is the St Joseph of Cluny convent. Dick Belton, her father, had been born there but qualified in medicine and for a few years specialised in tropical medicine in London. Dick was the eldest of four boys. There was just a year between him and his brother Jack, but twelve years between him and Paddy and thirteen years between him and Bobby. When the two younger boys were very young their father died and Dick Belton was made their guardian. As a result he had to give up medicine and come home to run the farm. She feels her father was never as fulfilled as he would have been if he'd continued in medicine. He married her mother, Freda who was ten years his junior, also a doctor, although she didn't practise after their marriage.

Of the four Belton brothers, Jack and Paddy subsequently became Lords Mayor of Dublin. Dick served on Dún Laoghaire Corporation for over forty years and was also a senator. Politics, she says, coursed in her father's veins but her mother had little interest and there was little political discussion at home. At times, she says, her mother felt it consumed her husband's life a little too much. Avril's grandmother, however, was very involved in her husband's political career. 'Old Paddy Belton', as he was known, was also a Lord Mayor of Dublin. He had met Michael Collins when they were both in the Geraldine GAA Club in London. Avril's grandmother had four sons but was 'not one to sit dangling a baby on her lap'. She was always at her husband's side at church gate meetings and was very much an independent-minded woman.

Avril is the eldest of five children. She says she had a very liberal upbringing and there was never any pressure to think in a particular way. The same was expected of the girls as of the boys in her family and they were all encouraged to go to third level. She says she was a fairly rebellious teenager and remembers what she calls 'a few turbulent years'. She decided to go to boarding school for her last three years and says she was very happy there. She loved the fun with her schoolmates and didn't feel in any way restricted. She had a very good headmistress who influenced her a lot, an Anglican minister's daughter who joined the Catholic Church, then joined the convent and within six years was reverend mother of Holy Child convent, Killiney. A woman with a worldly over-view she was very liberal in her attitude to teenage girls. Her idea of punishing Avril was to get her do something constructive; in the end she made her head of the class which, Avril says, transformed her. It just channelled all her enthusiasm. She had no problem taking responsibility or exercising authority. In fifth year Avril Doyle discovered there was a lot of satisfaction to be had out of academic achievement. She got a very good Leaving Certificate and considered doing medicine. Her father was dubious about her staying power and both her parents dissuaded her. Half afraid they might be right about the number of years involved in studying medicine she decided to do science, majoring in biochemistry.

She describes her time in University College Dublin (UCD) as the best years of her life. There was no responsibility, she lived at home and thoroughly enjoyed herself. She joined the Simon Community which she was introduced to by her brother Patrick who had just joined the Labour Party. However, Avril chose Fine Gael. It was the first time in her life that she had shown any interest in politics. She joined the universities' branch, which covered UCD and Trinity College Dublin (TCD).

Her father, she recalls, had a great interest in those who couldn't fight their own cause, 'not the person who was always banging on the door looking for more than they were entitled to,' she says. She describes him as very egalitarian in his outlook and almost a socialist in his principles. Equal opportunity in life is something she speaks passionately about. 'I'm all for the private sector, all for achievement, all for the best reaching the top. But I think equal opportunity must be given to all children right from the day they're born, equal opportunity under the health system, under the education system, regardless of their parents' income.' This is what motivates her in politics. She says that by nature human beings are not equal. There are those who will reach the top and £50,000 a year and those who will remain on the factory floor. But they should have been given an equal opportunity in society all along to develop their full potential. She is very much in favour of meritocracy. She admits to inheriting these feelings, to some extent, from her father but today they are very much her own views. She describes how she fully supports private medicine because those who can afford it *should* pay for themselves, so they are less of a burden on the tax-payer. But only the surroundings and the hospital should be different. The quality of medical treatment and the rate of access should not be different. Medical needs should dictate the speed at which surgery is done, not whether one can pay or not. This is why she loves local government; it's at the coal face of activity.

She says it is hard for women to get elected to Leinster House. The whole place is run to suit the male agenda. No matter what strides are made in terms of equality, at the end of the day the mother is still primarily responsible for the children, for their education, getting the meals on the table, making sure the school uniform is ready for Monday morning, making sure the homework is done, bringing the children to the doctor, sorting out all the problems that arise. There is a sort of natural focus towards the mother. Whether the woman is working or not doesn't matter. Avril feels that unless one is financially secure it's a pointless venture for a woman from a rural constituency to set her sights on the Dáil. It's easier if she is from a Dublin constituency; a long distance from Leinster House to home makes the logistics very difficult. National politics is very difficult for a mother of small children and there isn't equality of access. Even through the traditional entry point to politics of local government, there isn't equality of opportunity. There's no reason, she says, why married women, women with small children, shouldn't play a role in local government when they're only away for a few hours and the meeting is only down the road; they don't have to drive two hundred miles: they aren't away from home at night. She suggests women's lack of visibility at this level might be because there are not sufficient role models; women at local level are not participating in great enough numbers to encourage others to follow suit. She believes that until the problem of women's representation is solved at local level it will never be solved at national level. Local government is still the best school for national government. It hardens the neck and people learn to become comfortable with the abuse, and the whole ambiance of the debating arena. There's a huge job to be done, she feels, in equalising access.

Avril Doyle is a very assertive person. It doesn't bother her that some people find her arrogant and intimidating. When they get to know her they don't find her so, she says. There's a perception of Avril and then there's the real Avril. That's something about which she feels she has to be conscious in Wexford as well as in Leinster House. She says she gets on extremely well with her constituents from all walks of life, once they've actually met her. Those who haven't met her, she feels, think she's 'a bit Dublin four-ish'. It's a perception, one which she hopes doesn't match reality. She says that those who regard her as 'uppity and not knowing how the other half lives' simply don't know her. She enjoys her clinics where the vast majority of those who come to her are women who have never felt comfortable approaching a male politician and who just aren't getting the health treatment or other benefits to which they are entitled.

She says she has had quite a few moments of self doubt but maybe they don't show. To be successful one has to camouflage or compensate for just this. She feels she compensates for her inadequacies by assuming an air of being in control. This air of self-assuredness can be a defence mechanism. She finds work great therapy as well as great pleasure. She's a rigorous person but her favourite recreation is pursuing her interest in horses and ponies. She has no difficulty in closing her door at the weekend.

Avril Doyle was Junior Minister at the Office of Public Works for a year. She thoroughly enjoyed it. She loves the agenda of the environment and feels very strongly about it. She doesn't particularly remember the low points in her career but says the worst must have been when she lost her Dáil seat in 1989. She loved the Seanad campaign and the three-and-a-half years she spent there. She says she knows the relevance of the Seanad has to be measured against the Dáil but she found the level of debate there much better than that of the Dáil and enjoyed the greater freedom to tease out a point with a minister there. With her name suggested by some as next leader of Fine Gael, politics will continue to be Avril Doyle's passion for the foreseeable future.

Breeda Moynihan-Cronin

First elected to Dáil Eireann:
November 1992 — Labour Party

For Breeda Moynihan-Cronin politics is the family firm. Her father, Michael Moynihan, first stood for election for the Labour Party in South Kerry in 1954 when Breeda was just one year old. He finally took a seat in 1981. In November 1992 Breeda was concerned about three things when she started her campaign; would her father's vote transfer to her; would the women's vote materialise; did she have her own identity? As a seasoned campaigner, she knew after five or six days that she was going to make it to the Dáil. While the Spring factor (the popularity of Dick Spring nationally) was undoubtedly there, it was the Moynihan name in South Kerry that did the trick.

Breeda Moynihan-Cronin says nothing has ever intimidated her in her life. To sit in the Dáil chamber for the first time was fantastic. 'I was doing it for my father. I was so glad that he and my mother were alive to see that after all their hard work and their struggle he can still be involved in politics in his retirement years.' She remembers the bad days, all the years they were defeated. She says that her father's first election was a bigger thrill for her than winning her own seat. He now says he's not retired; he was made redundant by his daughter.

Michael Moynihan still has a constituency office in Killarney. His daughter says he was always a role model for her because she and her family looked up to him. Other people's fathers went to work and then went home, but Michael Moynihan always seemed to be doing things for people. He had his name in the paper and whenever dignitaries came to Killarney her parents were invited to meet them. She says she has a seasoned politician at her side for advice at least for her first few years as a national politician.

Both Breeda's parents were psychiatric nurses, as was her grandfather and as is her husband, Dan Christopher (known as D. C.) Cronin. For Breeda's mother, Mai, her family was her life. She wasn't particularly political but was very supportive of her husband. Breeda says her mother had to be at home when they were growing up because Michael was then a member of the Executive of the Irish Transport and General Workers' Union (ITGWU) and he had to go to Dublin quite a lot for meetings. There was no Labour vote in South Kerry then, but Breeda was reared on names like Dan Spring and Jack Harte. There were no party funds and Michael Moynihan had to fund all his election campaigns out of his own wages while also rearing his family of three boys and two girls. Breeda is very quick to point out that the family never went short. One of the difficulties her father faced was the fact that he was a county council employee and as such couldn't contest local elections. He had to wait until the health boards became independent. Not having a local council seat made it all the harder for him to win a Dáil seat. She remembers going to school when he had lost yet another election but says he never let it get him down; the fight for the next election began the day after the count. Her father was very protective of his family and kept a line drawn between them and his public life. For Breeda he was the voice of those who hadn't a voice.

Schooling for Breeda, the second eldest Moynihan, took place at the local primary and secondary school in Killarney. She wasn't particularly interested in the academic side of school but loved her friends and the camaraderie of school. Breeda wanted to be a domestic science teacher when she was young – she certainly had no ambitions to go into politics. Her mother put her name down for Sion Hill, the domestic science teacher-training college in Dublin, but she hadn't done science at school and so couldn't do the full course. However, she did a year at St Ann's in Sion Hill. She then went to Skerries Commercial College and ended up working in the bank. She remembers she went to the interview without a bag or gloves, in a green midi coat. She borrowed a bag and gloves from someone else at the interview. Breeda got the job. She was posted to Kildare and arrived in the town, knowing nobody, and with nowhere to stay. She went in to the first hotel she saw but didn't like the look of it or the people in it. 'She ended up in another hotel where she lived for about two months and then she shared a flat. Breeda says she cried the first night she arrived in Kildare but it was nothing to the way she cried when she left six years later. Her big interest in life at that stage was drama, although she always went home for election campaigns in spite of the bank's attitude that staff shouldn't be involved in politics. 'I brought John B to Kildare,' she says referring to John B Keane's plays. 'We did all his plays.' She made her own of *Big Maggie* and toured the country as part of the amateur dramatic scene. Subsequently, she started a drama group in Castleisland, Co. Kerry and with a number of others established a local theatre there.

For Breeda, life is about politics and people. She says there were always people in need around her father and those who supported her father were decent people. These facts greatly influenced her own decision to become involved in politics, although she says it really happened by default. Breeda married in 1983. Her husband was a Fianna Fáil supporter when she first met him. She says he wouldn't even give Labour a number twenty on the ballot paper then. He's now a member of the Labour Party and even his father canvasses for Labour now. In 1989 she gave up her job in the bank. At the time she was working in Kenmare and felt the difficulty of travelling the distance to and from Killarney. Also the tax burden she shared with her husband meant it wasn't worthwhile for both of them to work. When her father came back into the Dáil in 1989 he was in his seventies. Breeda decided to drive him around and help with his clinics. In the local elections of 1991 she was added to the Labour Party ticket by party head office. She won a county council seat and started to build for a Dáil seat. Two years earlier she would never have thought of a Dáil seat. When she won the council seat she had no idea that the Dáil seat would come so soon. The bug, she says, had hit by that stage.

She was doing thirty clinics a month and saw what was going on in the community. Many of the people in rural Ireland, she says, have no access to information and aren't aware of their rights. This is particularly true of women. She says women talk to her about things that she can't resolve in Leinster House. They talk to her just because they want to talk to someone. They come in and the tears flow but they go out with a smile on their face. She feels very strongly that support services must be established for people in difficulties. She speaks of girls who've told her they've been raped but that in Killarney there's no place for them to go. A lot of the doctors are male and the girls often don't have the money to pay for a doctor's visit. Breeda Moynihan-Cronin says she's not a qualified counsellor and qualified staff will have to be made available. She says she is liked by the people and known by them, she's the person they went to school with and they know they can trust her.

Despite the pressure of holding over thirty clinics Breeda Moynihan-Cronin still manages to enjoy life. She loves the races and she and her husband go frequently. They don't bet much money, not more than ten pounds a day, but they will often travel to a meeting and perhaps stay overnight. She came to enjoy the races when she lived in Kildare, but she doesn't go to the Derby anymore. 'I've turned off the Derby. I like the national hunt. I like to go where I wear the wellingtons and the coat. Although I like the glamour of the Derby, I feel the glamour has taken over from the racing. They're selling drinks for two-pounds-fifty in plastic glasses. Give me Thurles any day for a bowl of soup,' she quips. She loves walking and is determined that she will walk for an hour a day while in Leinster House. She has already started. She misses the fresh air of Kerry where she lives under the shadow of the mountains at Muckross. She finds the air in Leinster House 'fierce oppressive'. When she had the time she loved to cook and entertain but does little of this now. She's a creative cook and doesn't use recipes. Her husband too loves food and is a very good cook. As they don't have children and due to the hours her husband works as a psychiatric nurse, she hopes he'll be able to come to Dublin with her some of the time.

She says she feels no resentment at the amount of time politics now takes up in her life. Her father always wanted her to go into politics. She had felt, growing up, that there was no way she was going to have so-and-so knocking at her door at night. She remembers one by-election her father lost by forty-seven votes. They had no tally people and her father didn't look for a recount. She and her brother decided to build a tally team. Today they have one of the best. In November she got 7,524 votes; her tally people were only out by one vote. The Moynihan team is stronger and better organised than ever before in South Kerry. At the moment she is converting her garage into a constituency office where her husband will help out with her clinics. He had the last word on whether or not she would run for the Dáil. He's taken very well to it and she hopes that will last. When she sat in the county council beside Dick Spring she felt confident. Being elected with thirty-two other Labour TDs has made her very proud. She feels the twenty women TDs will have an impact in the 27th Dáil. She says she doesn't think of herself as a great success, what she wants to do is to be able to advance and improve her county and her country. Above all she would like to have a say in social welfare. It's the one area, she feels, which needs to be kept under review at all stages. She's looking forward to the next four years and feels that if the country isn't 'turned around' in that time it never will be. If it cannot be, Breeda Moynihan-Cronin will be one of those most disappointed and surprised.

Mary Wallace

First elected to Dáil Eireann:
June 1989 — Fianna Fáil

Mary Wallace describes herself as a conservative. Her fundamental values concern protection of the family, women and children in particular. She says that a combination of her convent education and her family background has made her conservative. She feels very strongly from a pro-life stance about the equal right to life of the foetus. She says she will have difficulty voting for abortion of any type in the future. But she is also very interested in any life-threatening situation faced by a woman and, if it were her own situation and there was a choice between her life and that of an unborn child, she agrees that she, the mother, would need protection. This is why she favoured the wording of the substantive issue in the November 1992 abortion referendum. She felt it gave protection to the woman *and* the unborn child. She does not favour allowing the threat of suicide as grounds for abortion. If such legislation is introduced, she feels it will diminish the kind of values that she upholds, and would open the door to abortion in this country.

Mary's brother is married and lives in the United States. She has visited him a number of times and talks of what she has seen as the type of society which comes from not having respect for the family unit. She thinks that the next generation must be protected, and she wants to preserve for them a strong set of family values. She has never had fundamental doubts about her conservatism. She looks at the opinion polls, looks at what other people are saying, looks at what feminist groups are saying and reads all documentation to inform herself. She still comes back to the belief that if basic values are kept everything else will fall into place.

She was born in Dunboyne, the second eldest of four children. Her father, Tom Wallace was a Fianna Fáil councillor from 1967 until his death in 1981. But he was never elected to the Dáil, having failed to get a nomination in the 1977 general election.

Growing up at home she had shares in some of the dogs and calves. It provided both interest and pocket money for herself and her brother and sisters. She also remembers hay-making in the summer and driving tractors. When Mary was twelve the family moved to Ratoath, Co. Meath, where in addition to the farm they had a shop and filling station where they all worked together. There was an annual family holiday, to Butlins, in Mosney Co. Meath, or

Skerries Co. Dublin or maybe Galway for the races. Her father was a bookmaker at Fairyhouse race-course at Easter, Punchestown race-course in May and Galway race-course in September.

Mary was sent to school as a boarder in Loreto convent, Balbriggan, Co. Dublin, which she enjoyed and which helped to make her more independent. She was a reasonably good student at school and she enjoyed sports.

Her father was very involved in farming organisations and chaired the Meath County Committee of Agriculture. He was a small farmer and he also did milk deliveries for the local community. Both Tom and Rosemary Wallace were very family-oriented. They seldom went out in the evening. She remembers her father getting up to collect milk churns at 4.00 am. He also trained greyhounds, something Mary loved to do with him; indeed she had been out walking the dogs with him on the morning of the day he died. Mary was working in Blanchardstown Hospital, Co. Dublin, at this stage. Her parents were due to go to the races that day. Her father went on ahead, had a heart attack and was brought to Blanchardstown where he died.

Mary was co-opted to her father's county council seat after his death. She says she was frequently shocked by what she heard in her clinics in those early years. The trauma and abuse of people particularly shocked her. Her clinic breakdown in gender terms was fifty per cent men and fifty per cent women. Men came for advice on business issues, planning and taxation questions while women, especially women who'd been separated, came about what she calls the 'worrying issues of life', like the medical card, mortgage and housing or marriage difficulties.

In 1985 Mary decided to seek a Dáil nomination for the general election. She was different in a number of ways to the other candidates. She was a young woman, located in John Bruton's end of the constituency. She says she had no great difficulty getting a nomination but fighting the election was an entirely different matter. In this multi-seat constituency, Mary Wallace says there is intense competition with 'your own', referring to members of her own party. She speaks of being judged by the supporters of another candidate in Fianna Fáil who took a dislike to her, although they'd never met her, because she was competition for 'their man'. It's something she has clearly experienced. She was seen by some as 'getting in the way', while her own supporters in her end of the constituency felt she could make it for them and they could back her.

She was devastated when she wasn't elected in 1987. It was devastating because the campaign had gone well. 'We had a marvellous team on the road,' she says. 'We had been working for two years from 1985 for it. Everything just seemed to go right.' On the election night her whole team felt they'd done well. When the first boxes at the count were opened things still looked good. Eventually she lost the seat by three hundred votes, a result which she squarely blames on lack of transfers from party colleagues. 'My whole life stopped when I lost,' she says. 'At one stage I was about to become a TD, I had worked a hundred hours a week up until now for this. It was more or less stolen from me by such a small portion of the vote. I felt very hard done by for my supporters. I felt stabbed in the back by some of my own.'

At that stage, she felt she would never get elected. She didn't feel personally put down by the result because her local vote was so strong. She went back to work in Blanchardstown Hospital, but decided to run for the Seanad. She felt she had little chance of election. She left work each evening at five o'clock and she canvassed until eleven o'clock at night, grabbed fish and chips and hit bed at three in the morning. The same pattern was repeated day after day. However, to her surprise, councillors greeted her with 'You're the girl from Co. Meath, from John Bruton's area; you did a great job.' Right up to the count she didn't expect to make it, but she did.

When the 1989 election arrived her attitude had

chang ... ↑ to win the seat and ran a
Mary ... ays politics hasn't made her
tough ... er wiser. When she finally
sat in ... ne, she thought about her
father. (... ection one of her father's
supporte ... g card from 1977. It was
when he ... nomination but didn't get
it. The s ...) Mary with her father's
signatur ... hat since 1977 he'd been
waiting f ... ted to the Dáil and asked
her to si ... ne says she found a great
sense of ... ther in the initial stages
because ... n his friends; they worked
with her.

Mary Wallace thinks it's very hard for a woman with no background in politics to break into this world. She points to the fact that of the five Fianna Fáil women TDs she is the only one who didn't have a parent or a grandparent in the Dáil. She says she's been very lucky to have the support of her mother and her fiancé, Declan Gannon. For a married woman with small children she sees enormous difficulties. 'I think women who can juggle the two (a Dáil seat and a family) are only marvellous.' She says she fell in love before she entered full-time politics. When she met Declan he had no interest in politics but now of all the people around her he is probably the most interested in political manoeuvres. She doesn't find that men are nervous of her because she's a politician. She doesn't expect to be treated differently, nor does she ask to be.

Entering politics so young has made her treat life very seriously. But she doesn't feel she's lost out on anything. She thinks TDs should lead by example; the electorate expects this of them. She regards the cynicism people feel about politicians as unfair and resents being tarred with the same brush as everyone else. She describes politics as the hardest career of all, but says it gives her a sense of achievement and while she's not into the power aspect of it, she does admit to being interested in a role in cabinet.

Mary agrees that at thirty-four everything in her life is dominated by politics. 'You can't decide to get married in the middle of an election campaign,' she says and so, while Mary and Declan have been engaged for some time, there is no date set as yet for the wedding. The same goes for when it comes to having children: all going well, she would try to plan a family for the start of a Dáil recess. Family is number one but she wants to ensure a balance, having family activities at an appropriate time of the year when politics doesn't interfere. She's not sure that it's worth having one's calendar dictated to by the political schedule but feels it's part of the job and she knew that when she went into it. Deputy Mary Wallace is sure of one thing. If her husband was to decide *he* couldn't take the pressure of her political life anymore after they're married, she would definitely put the family first.

Mary Coughlan

First elected to Dáil Eireann:
February 1987 — Fianna Fáil

When asked why she's involved in politics and a TD Mary
Coughlan is completely up front. 'I like to be on the inside
track. I get a great buzz from it. I like the sense of power,
the relative power that you have. I like being known. I like
going into Richard Alan's to buy a suit and feeling half
way guilty and at the same time knowing I really need it.'

She likes her party being in government because it means that she can have access to the Taoiseach and government ministers. But she also speaks of how she was attracted by the tradition and gut feeling of being in politics. For Mary Coughlan, taking on the mantle of Fianna Fáil had a very specific meaning. When she sought the nomination to stand for Fianna Fáil in Donegal South West she was just twenty-one years old, but she felt she owed it to her family, the family name and the local organisation to do so.

Mary's entry to the Dáil was the result of extremely tragic circumstances. Although her father was a member of the local branch of Fianna Fáil, politics didn't seriously impinge on her until her uncle was elected a TD in a by-election in 1980. Just three years after his election Clement was killed driving to Dublin for a meeting of the Fianna Fáil Parliamentary Party – a meeting at which Charles Haughey's leadership was being challenged. While her uncle was in favour of removing Charlie Haughey he knew the local party wanted him to support the leader. Mary says Clem Coughlan wanted to represent a new era in politics, but he also wanted to represent the people who had elected him. Clement was only forty years old and had seven children. Mary's father was approached by the constituency to run. Haughey arranged to meet him at the Ard Fheis and he too asked her father to stand in the by-election. Cathal Coughlan finally agreed to contest the convention. He won the nomination. Mary clearly remembers what he told the meeting. He was assuming his brother's mantle but not his brother's role. They were two entirely different people. But three years after romping home in the by-election Cathal Coughlan got cancer. At forty-eight years of age, he died in June 1986, just two months before Mary, the eldest of his seven children, did her final exams in Social Science in University College, Dublin (UCD).

Fianna Fáil turned to Mary's mother but she refused to stand. It was then Mary's turn. She thought a lot about her decision and finally said she might as well take the first bite of the cherry because, if she didn't, the cherry might be taken away. She was already involved in politics. She'd joined the Kevin Barry Cumann in UCD and was also active in Ogra Fianna Fáil, the party's youth section. She was used to visiting her father in Leinster House and had helped him with his correspondence. She had also helped out during the years when her uncle was a TD. She was very aware of being just twenty-one. She knew that it was an awful life in which she would have little time for herself and would always be under pressure, at everyone's beck and call. She contested the convention for her father's county council seat first, but let it be known at the time that she would be seeking the Dáil nomination. There were two others contesting but she won. She says she didn't find it that difficult to ask for support. They had all known her father well. She was co-opted not just to his seat on the council but to all his committee positions, so she became vice chairperson of the Vocational Education Committee (VEC) on her first day in the council. It was a position she loved. She says she was never as nervous in her life as when she contested the convention for the 1987 election. She spent days preparing her speech. She defeated two others for the nomination, and topped the poll in the general election. She was the youngest TD ever elected, just a couple of months younger than Síle de Valera had been in 1977. She's convinced that being both young and a woman really helped her.

The day she took her seat she remembers standing at the bottom of the stairs leading up to the Dáil chamber. She was terrified. 'There was a whole gang of people up from Donegal and I remember feeling, "Oh my God what am I going to do?" ' She remembers the crowds, the noise, everybody pretending they knew what they were doing. Her constituency colleague, Pat the Cope Gallagher, was very good to her and got her started. She quickly found out that everybody was on their own and that it was a very competitive place, not just between deputies in the same constituency but between constituencies. She describes life in Leinster House as very lonely. There are very few young TDs, 'and you can't really be going out with the lads,' she says. She socialises very little with politicians. Most she describes as associates, few as friends. Single men, especially in her constituency, are afraid of her, she says, apart from those she's known over the years. She regards this as a huge problem 'because everybody talks about you'. So she has tended to do most of her socialising in Dublin. She mentions the complete lack of even basic private facilities in Leinster House. In the last Dáil she shared an office with Dick Roche and had to hunt him out of the room if she was going out and needed to change her clothes. 'There are no facilities for women in this place. There's nowhere to sit if you have a headache, nowhere for a pregnant woman to lie down, especially a rural TD, who can't go home.'

Mary did manage to meet and fall in love with her husband, David Charlton, in Leinster House. She met him in April 1989. It was a Thursday evening when they met casually, she was picking up her post, he was a Garda about to go off duty and he asked her to meet him for a drink. The general election intervened, but when she returned to the House they started seeing each other again. Trying to maintain their privacy was very difficult, so they tended to go to places where other politicians wouldn't be. They went to the Garda Club a lot and essentially went out with his friends most of the time. Within a year they were married. Mary and her husband would like to have a family but she talks of the problems that poses for a rural TD. 'It will cause a terrible strain. It's very difficult to be married, not to talk of having a family.' She says that everyone's marriage is difficult no matter what. Her husband works shifts in Glenties, Co. Donegal, and she's in Dublin for most of the week. She says having a family would place a tremendous financial burden on them because they would have to employ full-time help. She has the added disadvantage of representing one of the most distant constituencies from Leinster House. To shorten the long drive to the Dáil Mary also drives through the North, but says she never drives near an RUC car in case it's a target. She sometimes checks with the Gardaí about the route she might take on particular occasions. There are times when she resents the intrusion politics makes on her private life and she would love to give it all up some days. Even when she's at home she's only in the door and then out again. She can already see the toll this life has taken on some of her colleagues.

It's been a long road for Mary Coughlan since she was taught first by her Uncle Clem in Frosses National School near Donegal town, and then in fourth, fifth, sixth and seventh class by the master, her father, Cathal. She now knows that she has to fight to retain her seat in spite of the huge level of support there is for Fianna Fáil in Donegal South West. She's had to struggle to be accepted for herself. 'I hate when people say, "Well if your father was alive he'd have got this done." ' The difference, she says, when both her uncle and her father were in Leinster House was that there was money being spent by government. This is not happening in the 1990s.

Regarded as 'a little kid' when she was elected, she says at times she played up on that. When she knew she could get something out of a minister because she was the same age as his daughter she said, 'Right, I'm going to try and get something out of these guys.' A lot of people found if very difficult because she was the same age as their daughters and sons, yet here she was talking to them on the same level. It was difficult for her constituents to come to her at a clinic. Many still tend to feel that she's not really in the middle of it all. She says she is a good lobbyist but that hasn't helped her public image. She claims there are times when she can't be in the Dáil. She may have a company on whose behalf she's negotiating with a state agency; it may not even be known about and there's no public credit for this. That's Irish politics at present, she says.

Mary Coughlan hates speaking in the Dáil chamber. She likes to think she knows what she's talking about and says it takes her too long to prepare. Women deputies, she says, are more concerned about knowing what they're talking about. But she feels she's going to have to do something about this problem and thinks the proposed new committee system will help.

Mary would love to serve in a ministerial capacity at some stage and says she would love to get back into Agriculture and Fisheries. She came in to Leinster House and learned to be a TD; she has no overt ambition and says maybe that's a problem. Mary Coughlan is not sure if she's in politics for life. On a good day she loves it. She enjoys the hard work. She doesn't mind going to meetings. She loves being part of politics and participating. But on bad days she wonders what she's doing in Leinster House. On such days she feels she has ruined her life and that at twenty-seven years of age she feels like sixty. However, her good days far outnumber her bad ones.

Máire Geoghegan-Quinn

First elected to Dáil Eireann:
March 1975 — Fianna Fáil

Máire Geoghegan-Quinn has made a very important decision about her future. She has thought about it long and hard and is determined that when Albert Reynolds retires she is going to stand for leader of Fianna Fáil. She doesn't expect him to retire in the near future but says that, unlike Charles Haughey, he'll know when to go. She feels that unlike the last leadership contest in 1992, Fianna Fáil will then be ready for a woman leader.

Certainly she is no stranger to the corridors of power. She first came to Dublin in Gerald Bartley's, her godfather's, state car, when she was just four years old. He was Minister for Defence at the time and in his office they put her in a tea chest to keep her quiet. 'I was obstreperous even then,' she says. At fifteen she was addressing after-mass meetings for her father, Johnny Geoghegan TD who was parliamentary secretary in the Department of Social Welfare before his death in 1975. He had made no secret of the fact that he considered Máire to be the politician of the family and that he would like her to take his seat. As a school-girl in the Mercy Convent in Tourmakeady she was very much involved in debating. He encouraged her and regarded it as great training for politics, even when she was debating against government policy.

Her father was very good with people, 'much better than I'll ever be,' she says modestly. He drove the CIE bus from Galway to Carna. This was how he met her mother, a schoolteacher, and when they married they lived in Carna until 1970 when they moved into Galway City because her brother, a diabetic, needed to be near a hospital. Máire says that when her father was a councillor he was chosen by Gerald Bartley to stand for the party in Connemara because of his popularity in the area. Máire's earliest memories are of him getting up at five o'clock on Tuesday mornings, driving to Galway for the Dublin train to go to Leinster House, and returning on Thursday nights.

There were always people at their house, not just because her father was a TD but because they had one of the few telephones in the area. People in Connemara, she says, were self-sufficient. They did some fishing, they grew their own vegetables. Her memories of families at the time were of men and women working hard together. Women did as much work as men. They controlled the purse strings and decided how money would be spent and on what. Máire Geoghegan grew up with an image of women being strong. Her mother had given up her career only because of the marriage bar. She felt strongly about that and, had she been able to work she would have done so. Her father, Máire says, would have had no choice in the matter but probably would have been happy about it. Máire's mother always encouraged her to become educated for a job. It was the same ethos at school where there was never a question of being educated to be someone's wife. It was very much an emphasis on future career.

Although Máire thought of going into politics all through school and during her years of teacher training in Carysfort College, she gave up the idea when she married. She had been in a very serious relationship which broke up in 1970. She says she was in a bit of a rut when her best friend suggested coming to stay with her in Tuam for a weekend. On the Saturday they went to a dance in the Las Vegas Ballroom. Máire says a guy came in to the hall who was so tall and so skinny that he stood out from everybody else. He eventually asked her up. She told him she couldn't jive and he said, 'Well you're going to learn.' The guy was John Quinn. She didn't tell him who her father was for some time. He had a hang-up that she was socially more advantaged than he was. When she did tell him he wanted to break it off. But when John met her father they got on like a house on fire. 'They were both full of devilment,' she recalls.

They got married in 1973 and their first child Rory was born in 1974. Máire was teaching in Galway at the time. She had what she calls a stereotyped image of herself, an idea that it was fine having a job provided you were home every night. Her father died tragically of a heart attack in 1975 and Fianna Fáil came to the family to talk about it, and targeted her to replace him because she was the one who had been involved in politics. She decided to stand. She went before a very tight convention, where she was opposed by five councillors. She's glad it was tough because it prepared her for the difficulties that arose for her later on. It also gave her the opportunity to really consider whether or not she wanted to do this. She drove around the constituency after school, seeking support. The main disadvantage she had was in convincing people that she could do the job as well as any man, coupled with the fact that she was young with a year-old son. They were concerned, she says, about whether or not she could give it the time it needed, questions they would never ask a man. She remembers with particular anger, being in the mortuary when her father died. Two of the councillors who were standing against her canvassed for votes within her hearing. She says she found it terribly sad. 'The man was only in the coffin. He hadn't even been buried and already he was gone, past and forgotten about.' But that, she says, is politics. The incident played a big role in her decision. It steeled her determination. She took the seat in the by-election.

Within two years she was appointed a parliamentary secretary by Jack Lynch. The first she knew of it was when the Taoiseach announced it in the Dáil. She met Gerry Collins and asked him if he knew where she was going. He wouldn't tell her where but said, 'You're getting the toughest minister of all.' The minister in question was Des O'Malley and she says the two years she worked with him were two of the best of her career. 'He was generous with his time. He was generous with the work of the department.' She dealt with Consumer Affairs in Industry and Commerce. They put fourteen pieces of legislation through the House. Her second son Cormac was born in July 1979. She worked up until a week before his birth and had made a conscious decision that she was going to nurse him. In September she had a call from the minister who wanted to know when she was coming back to work. She told him she wanted to come back but could only do so if she had a facility to breastfeed Cormac. Arrangements were made for a small room beside her office to take the carry-cot. A student friend came in to look after him and whenever his time came for a feed (regardless of what his mother was doing), she got up, went to the room and fed him. 'He travelled the countryside with me. Every Tuesday morning I packed Cormac, carry-cot, nappies into the car. He was fed in the state car on many an occasion.' She says it was a very happy time for her although looking back on it she doesn't know how she managed. Her colleagues were not particularly interested. One person who did inquire after her constantly, however, was Charles Haughey who was Minister for Health at the time. Nobody in Leinster House saw the baby, though. He stayed in his mother's office in Kildare Street. Now that there are twenty women in the Dáil, some of them of child-bearing age, should nursing facilities become an issue, there will be a great network of women to support a TD doing the same thing, she says.

When Charles Haughey replaced Jack Lynch as leader of Fianna Fáil Máire felt she might lose her place in government. For a couple of days friends had been ringing pretending to be the new Taoiseach. One morning as she had breakfast with John the phone rang and John said, 'Cop on! Who is it this time?' The voice at the other end said, 'This is Charlie Haughey.' He didn't say why he wanted to see her but when they met his words were, 'Well, Máire, I think you and I are going to make history.' She was to be the first cabinet minister since Constance Markievicz. When he asked her what she had to say she remembers asking, 'Well, am I good enough?' When she thinks back she kicks herself. 'Only a woman would say that and only in 1979 would a woman say it. There's no way I'd say it now,' she says. He got very cross and told her he wouldn't have asked her if he didn't think she was good enough.

Máire Geoghegan-Quinn has been very hurt in politics. The worst years, she says, were 1981 and 1989. The first occasion was when her home was picketed by Fianna Fáil members during factory closures when she was in Industry and Commerce. Her son asked, 'Why do they all hate you, Mom?' That, she thought, was terrible. It was an

147

invasion of privacy that hurt her deeply. These were people who had worked for her and were now saying dreadful things. Later in 1989 during the controversy concerning rod licences in two of the villages where she had always had great support she says people were vicious. Her children got abusive phone calls, her telephone line was cut. Rory was verbally abused in front of his schoolfriends by a woman, the partner of one of the leading lights of the Anti Rod Licence Campaign. She also had two particularly public political disappointments. It's interesting, she says, that the same individual, Pádraig Flynn, was involved in both. He replaced her in the Department of the Gaeltacht when Charles Haughey dropped her from cabinet. He was the person Albert Reynolds appointed European Commissioner when she wanted the job. She says these things are part of politics; she refuses to dwell on them. 'If you start having resentments against people it eats you up. It's not bothering them. They don't care whether you're resentful or not.' In relation to the Commissioner's job she says she also had to decide whether or not to uproot her whole family or leave them behind. She doesn't deny wanting it, but says she couldn't have been happier than when she was offered the Justice portfolio.

'It's a department that you wouldn't normally have a woman in,' she says. She feels, that just as when she became Minister for Tourism, Transport and Communications, she's breaking new ground. 'It's important,' she feels, 'that women aren't always slotted into the caring ministries.' She agrees that it's probably the most male of all departments. 'I don't know if they've come to terms with the fact that I'm there at all yet. I'm very different to the man who was there before me. I come in with a big liberal tag attached to me.' She's delighted that she's coming in with a new department secretary but she is disappointed that she won't be dealing with divorce. 'As somebody who found myself on the wrong side of these issues on so many occasions in Fianna Fáil I'm disappointed that I'm not going to be introducing this legislation,' she says. But she is very happy about the new Department of Equality and is particularly happy that she will be the one to decriminalise homosexuality. The day she arrived in the department she told the officials she intends having the legislation on the statute books before the summer.

The culture of the Department of Justice is very male-oriented but she hopes to see changes and has already been talking about 'pink ghettoes' and 'glass ceilings'. She says women gardaí have been writing to say how pleased they are that there's a woman minister saying positive things about women at every rank. In her former ministry she was extremely annoyed about the suggestion of 'hand-bagging' the Aer Lingus Board. She was unhappy with the answers she was getting from the board and decided to talk to them. 'I did what any male minister would have done. I spoke openly and frankly and I have a reputation for being straight and up-front.' As a result she was said to have hand-bagged the board. She made a decision to take on the hand-bagging issue but decided to do it on the floor of the Dáil. She prayed that someone would actually use the term. Austin Curry brought it up. 'He was just going to get hammered. It was as simple as that,' she says. She feels it was very important to do it because when it happened in Britain they were allowed to get away with it. It was looked on as a kind of a joke. It was important to make the point, she feels, not just for herself but for any woman who is making decisions.

Máire Geoghegan-Quinn knows she's regarded as cold and aloof. She says she minds her own business. She has lots of acquaintances but just a very small group of friends. That, she thinks, comes from the fact that she's had bad experiences and been hurt. Her best friend in politics is Pat the Cope Gallagher. He went to school with her brother, her husband became a business friend of his, and when she was Minister for the Gaeltacht and he was a councillor she had a lot of dealings with him. She says they often have mental telepathy. Any time she's felt down he either rings or appears in the door of her office. The same has happened for him. She gave the once-over to his girlfriends before he decided to get married and she was there to support him during the controversy over his decision to marry a woman who'd been jailed. 'He really is a great, great friend. He's my best buddy in politics.' That's very important, she feels, because people automatically assume that when a woman TD strikes up a friendship with a male colleague, there is something going on. It was one of the things she found hard to cope with when she first became a minister and had to take semi-state executives or board members out to dinner. Inevitably, innuendo and comment was made. It used to bother her terribly until one day she said, 'Men are doing this every day of the week, I'm not going to worry about it.'

Máire Geoghegan-Quinn did have one crisis in her marriage. It came in 1987. Involvement in politics, she says, puts pressure on everybody's marriage and the fact that she's been a member of government for so long and so consumed with her work put extra pressure on hers. But, any job that takes people away from home does the same thing. She says both she and John worked through it and their relationship has been strengthened. It has helped her to re-order priorities in her life and to realise that at the end of the day you only have one person, your best friend. Talking of that difficult period, Máire says, 'You hope that you are married to your best friend. In my case I am.'

Mary Harney

First elected to Dáil Eireann:
June 1981 — Progressive Democrats

'My mother takes the view, even now, "It's a pity you don't get a proper job." She thinks this is a dreadful life.'

Mary Harney has been an Oireachtas member for sixteen years. For much of that time she's been at the very cutting edge of Irish politics. Although she doesn't like to think she'll be in politics for the rest of her life, she would

151

like to be back in government but next time as a cabinet minister.

As Junior Minister for the Environment in the Fianna Fáil/Progressive Democrats government she was enormously frustrated. Junior ministers are not at the cabinet table where decisions are made, and so can't argue their own case. It can be extremely difficult to get access to ministers and, she says, juniors tend to get lobbed with a lot of the down-side problems. She thinks it's crucial to have a good and trusting relationship with the minister, something she enjoyed with Michael Smith and Rory O'Hanlon but definitely not with Pádraig Flynn.

On a personal level she says Flynn and she had quite a good relationship. She remembers another minister remarking how they got on so well together after seeing them at a dinner. But politically and work-wise she says, 'It was desperate.' She feels he genuinely finds it hard to work with women as equals or to take them seriously. It was no secret that he didn't like the coalition, and, she says, he fostered an air of mistrust and seemed determined that she wasn't going to get anywhere. She says she challenged him several times on these issues and remembers on one occasion, when they were having it hot and heavy, he told her she was just like his daughter. 'That really infuriated me. Not only was I being treated as someone who wasn't equal but as someone who was his daughter.' Mary Harney says that the only way they got business done was when the Taoiseach, Charles Haughey, intervened, which he did on a number of occasions. 'But you couldn't be going to him every day with problems or every week either. Any of the things that got done did so through Haughey's intervention,' she says.

Most people regard foreign travel as one of the perks of being in government. Not Mary Harney. For her, trips abroad, although they meant the best rooms in hotels, were times of real loneliness. Working lunches and dinners were fine, but when they were over she would read a book or a paper, listen to the radio or watch television and if she had to eat alone she would stay in the hotel rather than go out. The civil servants accompanying the minister would always want to include her when they were going out. But she felt she might be cramping their style since she was the boss and so, other than a couple of drinks or an occasional meal with them, she would retire. She herself was conscious of this, although, she says, they never made her conscious of it. Whenever she went to her room, she says, whether it was early or late, she was always aware of being lonely and she usually clocked up big phone bills to Ireland when she was away.

Mary Harney's political career began at the age of twenty-four when she was appointed to the Seanad by Jack Lynch in 1977. Contrary to some people's perception, that she was like a daughter to him, she had only met him about three times and didn't really know him at all. She had just recently graduated from Trinity College Dublin (TCD) where she had joined Fianna Fáil. She jokingly explains that when she joined the party half the Trinity *cumann* had just resigned over the Offences Against the State Act. She was made treasurer at her first meeting. She came from a Fianna Fáil background. Her father was a party activist. She has early memories of Kevin Boland visiting the house and she recalls distributing leaflets at election time. She says her family's politics obviously influenced her and a number of her friends were involved in politics, although several, like George Bermingham, were in Fine Gael. This was 1974 when Fianna Fáil was revamping its organisation and trying to attract young people, especially women, to the party. Mary began speaking at youth conferences. She was the first woman to be elected auditor of the History Society (The Hist), one of the most prestigious of university debating societies. She quickly gained a high media profile.

When Jack Lynch and Fianna Fáil swept to power in the 1977 election Mary was teased by her friends that she would be 'on the soccer team' and would get the call. Allusions to the Taoiseach's eleven nominees to the Seanad were constantly being made. She was working in United Dominion's Trust (UDT) as economic researcher on their client base, when she did indeed get a call. She picked up the phone to hear on the other end, 'Hello Mary. This is Jack Lynch. I'd like to nominate you to the Seanad. Will you accept?' She can't remember what she said other than yes.

When she took her seat she was extremely conscious of her age and felt a lot of people were wondering what the hell Jack Lynch was doing nominating someone so young. She didn't know many people in the party, thought she'd never master the procedure and was very intimidated. She felt somehow that she didn't merit being there. She remembers receiving her first pay cheque a month after her nomination and her parents's reaction when she opened the cheque for £101, saying it was great money. She'd been nominated in August, the Seanad had still to meet and she got the cheque in September although she hadn't yet done anything. Mary says her time in the Seanad was the only time she was really politically ambitious. She immediately set to work to win a local council and Dáil seat. She also says that Charlie Haughey, who was Minister for Health at the time, was the one minister who really made an effort to talk to her and be helpful. I asked her if she ever forgave him for the way in which he became Taoiseach. She says she forgives very easily but she never forgot the fact that he played a central role in the events leading to Jack Lynch's resignation and it coloured her relationship with him for a long time after. She'd really had a high regard for Jack Lynch. She says that when she joined the party the alternative to Lynch was Liam Cosgrave, whom she saw as conservative. She came to admire Lynch in a way she'll never admire anyone else.

Mary Harney's mother would have liked her eldest child to be a teacher and to marry. Teaching would have been a nice job. She would have been home at three o'clock and could have looked after her family. Mary did spend a year teaching but hated it. Although she's proud of her daughter, Mrs Harney still doesn't like her being a full-time politician. Above all she doesn't like the fact that she's alone and hasn't married. She still worries about Mary holding her seat and each election takes its toll on her.

Mary prefers to live alone. Privacy is very important to her and she enjoys her independence. When I asked her if she's a lonely person she replied, 'If I think about it, yes.' She doesn't allow herself think to about it. She rarely spends an evening alone at home unless she's got housework to do. On the rare occasion that she might finish work early she'd never go home at six o'clock and read a book or watch television. She says she needs people around her and probably travels in larger groups than most.

She says men find women in politics difficult to deal with. She feels she intimidates a lot of men. She thinks that to be successful in politics it is necessary to develop male habits. If you want to push something you're accused of being aggressive and that's not supposed to be a good thing for a woman. If you get upset and show it, in a way that a man doesn't, you're accused of being emotional. You can never win.

She has no doubt that the reason why she's still a single woman is because of her involvement in politics. When she went into politics she says it took over her whole life. She forgot about everything else. She gave it everything. Every night when her friends were going out she was working for a Dáil seat. Firstly, she had to get a nomination and then build up a base in Tallaght where she was totally unknown. So she put everything into politics in the years between twenty-four and twenty-eight, years which, she feels, are the best years in terms of relationship development.

She doesn't regret anything she did except that so many things happened to her when she was so young. She thinks she missed out on a huge chunk of her life. Not so much, she says, in terms of marriage, because she's not so sure if she'd want to marry at all, but she missed out on seriously considering it. She'd like to be in a permanent relationship but there's nobody with whom she'd wish it now. She says the option of having a permanent long-term relationship is a vague concept in the absence of someone specific but that given a choice, yes, she would like one. She thinks society is couple-centred. She's certain that being a woman on her own will inhibit her political progress and is definite that she will never go for leadership of the party (though she is deputy leader now). When colleagues try to convince her that that's where she should aim she says she wouldn't dream of it. The sense of responsibility for others, she says, is a thing she wouldn't like to take on alone. When you're a leader, she says, you're isolated, even from your colleagues. It's a very lonely, very isolated position. The idea of going home and being totally alone and not having anybody to toss things over with is bad. She says 'I see what a help Des O'Malley's wife Pat is to him and how dependent he is on her. I feel you don't have to be married to somebody, but the closeness of a permanent relationship is important. With it you don't feel that sense of isolation. If you have to go to a function, you're not on your own.' Mary Harney hates what she calls the embassy circuit, where you go on your own, you make small talk with people, you wander around for an hour and then you go home. But that's part and parcel of political life and when you're a leader it's so much more important. Without hesitation, she says this means she'll never be Taoiseach.

Mary is an impatient person. She never queues in the supermarket. While she wouldn't like to be in politics for the rest of her life, she says it's hard to re-motivate oneself to break into a new area. She'd like to go into business, not to make money but to have control. She says the worst part of politics is not being able to control your life and always having to think of other people.

She describes herself as the kind of person who 'shoots from the hip'. She knows what she thinks about most things and is very decisive. The fact that you have to be cautious in politics, that that's the number one rule of the game, she finds hard to take. Instinctively she's not a cautious person and she hates organised life. She gets bored very easily. She constantly wants to move on. To a certain extent she says this has been her attitude to relationships with men. It's the unknown that she finds exciting. Getting to know someone is what she likes most; once known, they tend to become boring. That, she feels, is part of the reason why her life isn't as fulfilled as it could be. She has friends who are much happier with an awful lot less than she has.

The approval of her parents is very important to Mary Harney. She says if she joined a communist party her mother would still support her. She recalls being worried when she was leaving Fianna Fáil, principally because of how her father would react. In comparison she wasn't a bit worried about whether she'd ever win a seat again.

She was in North America for two months before the Progressive Democrats were formed and thought all the time about how her exit from Fianna Fáil would affect her father. She discussed it with him when she'd actually made up her mind. He told her whatever she wanted to do he'd support her. She was deeply unhappy with herself before she left Fianna Fáil. She says that, if the Progressive Democrats hadn't happened, she'd have left politics. She began to feel there was no future for her there. During the various leadership battles in Fianna Fáil efforts were made, she says, to intimidate her. She could deal with that but she talks of anonymous phone calls made to her mother; these upset her deeply. Anonymous callers said she was an alcoholic, was having affairs with married men and was going to be killed on the Naas Road. She was very unhappy with Fianna Fáil's social conservatism. The number of times she voted in the Dáil in a way she knew was personally wrong got to her after a while. She became totally demotivated, deeply miserable and unhappy. Politics had been her whole life and suddenly she could see it all falling apart. That, she says, is why she put so much pressure on Des O'Malley to form the new party. 'I used every trick in the book to convince him,' she says.

Mary Harney doesn't worry much, although, as she says, with no permanent job and a huge mortgage she has lots to worry about. Her one regret is that she didn't become a barrister. She'd have liked the excitement of each new case. She enjoys power and feels having it is the only way you can do things. But she also feels it can corrupt people. She has no fear of taking people on or of making decisions. Politics, she says, is a very hard life and th[e] system can make good people into lesser people. She h[as] seen some very good people broken down by the who[le] political game. It's a rough trade, she concludes.